GEORGIAN BAY & COTTAGE COUNTRY

CAROLYN B. HELLER

Contents

GEORGIAN BAY & COTTAGE COUNTRY

Cottage Country

Look for ★ to find recommended
sights, activities, dining, and lodging.

Highlights

★ **Muskoka Wharf:** Learn how steamships helped develop tourism around the Muskoka Lakes at this Gravenhurst development that includes a historic boat museum, and cruise the lake on a traditional steamship (page 15).

★ **Canoeing in Algonquin Provincial Park:** Ontario's largest provincial park is one of the province's best destinations for canoeing, whether you're paddling on the numerous lakes and rivers or taking a multiday trip across the backcountry (page 29).

★ **Science North:** Sudbury's cool, contemporary science museum is filled with "please touch" exhibits that are particularly ecofriendly (page 37).

★ **Temagami:** This lake region is one of the most accessible places in the north for canoe trips, whether you're a novice or experienced paddler (page 39).

★ *Polar Bear Express* **Train:** Go where no roads go on this rail trip north to James Bay, where you can explore the Cree First Nations communities of Moosonee and Moose Factory Island (page 42).

For a getaway to the outdoors, head north to Ontario's Cottage Country and to the woodland region that extends northeast, all the way to James Bay.

The Muskoka Lakes region north of Toronto has long been a popular weekend getaway for families to escape to their summer cottages or stay at lakeside resorts. Muskoka Cottage Country begins just 100 kilometers (60 miles) north of Toronto and is centered around the towns of Gravenhurst, Bracebridge, and Huntsville. Dotted with inland lakes, ski hills, and waterfront towns along Lake Muskoka and numerous smaller lakes, this region offers plentiful opportunities for outdoor adventure and relaxation. The area's top attraction is Algonquin Provincial Park, one of Ontario's largest protected green spaces; visit for a day or a week and take a short hike, paddle across an inland lake, or set out on a multiday wilderness adventure.

Beyond Algonquin, smaller parks like Arrowhead Provincial Park are great for families looking to camp, hike, or swim, while farther north, the lakes and forests surrounding Temagami make it a prime destination for canoe trips.

While the northeast is a natural choice for outdoor adventures, it's ripe for cultural explorations, too. Aboriginal people have lived in Northern Ontario for thousands of years, and many First Nations welcome visitors who want to learn about their culture and traditions. If you venture north to the remote communities of Moosonee and Moose Factory Island on the shores of James Bay, you can explore the culture of the Cree First Nation, one of Canada's largest aboriginal groups.

Northeastern Ontario also has a large francophone population, so don't be surprised to see bilingual signs or hear *"Bonjour"* and *"Merci."* The city of Sudbury is particularly bilingual; it's Canada's third-largest French-speaking community outside Quebec. In some northern towns, you'll find French Canadian influences in the food, with *tourtière* (meat pie) and *poutine* (french fries topped with cheese curds and gravy) almost as common as burgers and fries.

Looking for outdoor adventure? Cultural adventure? Just plain adventure? Then head north.

Previous: canoeing on Ontario's northern lakes; Algonquin's Killarney Lodge. **Above:** The world's largest Muskoka chair welcomes visitors to Gravenhurst.

Cottage Country, Algonquin, and the Northeast

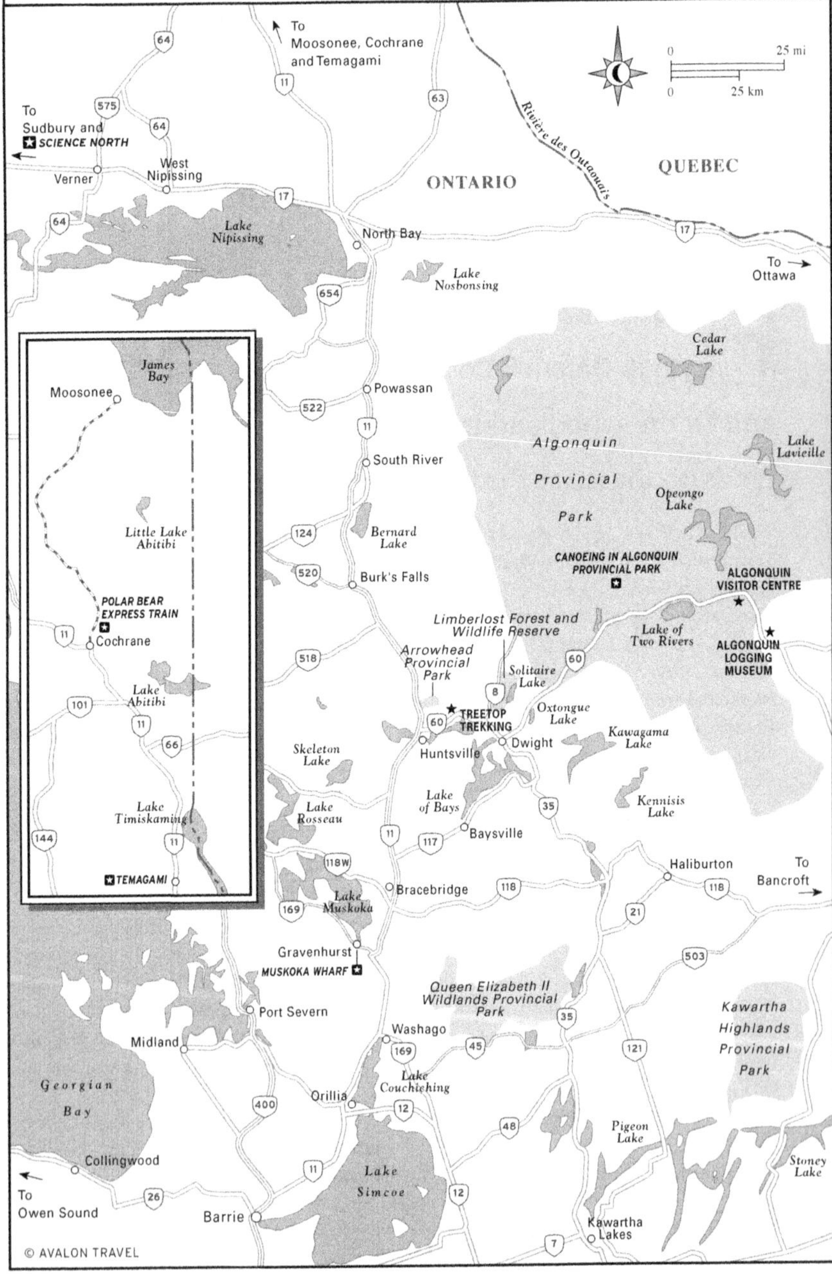

PLANNING YOUR TIME

This region is packed with outdoor activities, but many Cottage Country and northeastern attractions don't begin operation until mid- or late May and close in mid-October, after the Canadian Thanksgiving weekend. July and August are the busiest travel months; fall is the best time to visit, when the foliage is most dramatic.

A weekend trip could take you to the Muskokas and **Algonquin** for a relaxing outdoor getaway. You'd want at least a long weekend to take a canoe trip in **Temagami** or to explore the cities of North Bay or Sudbury. With several days to spare, you could travel to Cochrane, then take the ***Polar Bear Express* Train** onward to the Cree communities of **Moosonee** and **Moose Factory Island.**

Muskoka Cottage Country

With more lakes than you can count, the Muskoka region is one of Ontario's vacation lands. For many Ontarians, Muskoka is Cottage Country, a place to escape from the city, where your obligations are nothing more than to sit on the porch of your cottage and relax. Even people who don't have cottages of their own (or friends with cottages who invite them for weekends) head to Cottage Country to stay in B&Bs, hotels, or the many cottage resorts that dot the lakes.

The Muskoka region, north of Toronto, encompasses the towns of Gravenhurst, Bracebridge, and Huntsville, among others, extending northwest to Georgian Bay and northeast to Algonquin Provincial Park. Tourism to Muskoka began in earnest in the 1800s when steamboats transported visitors across the lakes. These days, nearly all the steamboats are gone (except for a couple used for sightseeing cruises), but the visitors continue to come. And if you're looking for a place to get outdoors, whether to hike, canoe, or just sit on the porch, you should, too.

BARRIE

Barrie isn't really part of the Muskoka region, but you'll likely pass through the city on your way north. Even though it's 105 kilometers (65 miles) north of Toronto, it feels

the mantra for summer in Ontario

Muskoka Lakes

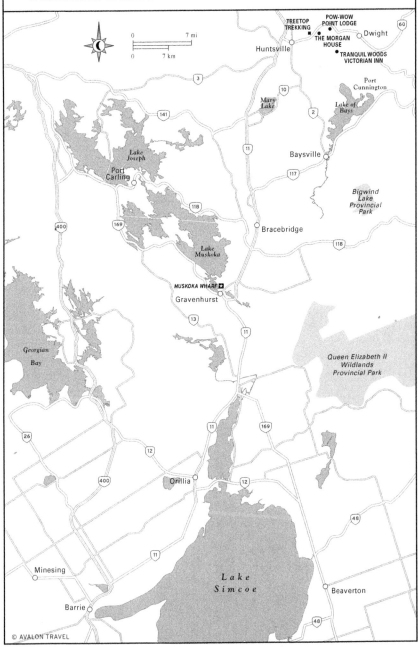

© AVALON TRAVEL

like an extension of the metropolitan area (and people do commute daily from Barrie to Toronto), rather than the start of a cottage holiday. Still, it's a handy spot to break up your drive, whether to have a bite to eat or to stay for a day or two. And if you're continuing north from Barrie, stop in the town of Orillia to tour the former home of noted Canadian humorist Stephen Leacock. Barrie spreads out along the shore of Lake Simcoe, so even in the heart of the city, you can stroll along the lake. Dunlop Street is the main downtown thoroughfare; most sights and shops are on or around Dunlop.

Barrie has a small but worthwhile art museum, the **Maclaren Art Centre** (37 Mulcaster St., 705/721-9696, www.maclarenart.com, 10am-5pm Mon.-Fri., 10am-4pm Sat.-Sun., adults $5), which exhibits work by established Canadian and emerging regional artists. Half of the building was Barrie's original public library, built in 1917; the other half is an airy contemporary addition. If you're looking for a gift for an arty friend, browse the jewelry and works by local artists in the gallery shop.

You can cruise the lake on the *Serendipity Princess* (Bayfield St., at Simcoe St., 705/728-9888, www.midlandtours.com, June-Sept., adults $26, seniors $24, students $21, ages 5-14 $16, families $68), a paddle-wheel boat that offers daily summer sightseeing excursions. Boats depart from the Barrie Town Dock.

If you're heading north and need outdoor gear, stop at the Barrie outpost of **Mountain Equipment Co-op** (61 Bryne Dr., 705/792-4675, www.mec.ca, 10am-7pm Mon.-Wed., 10am-9pm Thurs.-Fri., 9am-6pm Sat., 11am-5pm Sun.), a Canadian chain that stocks clothing, camping equipment, and other supplies. You must be a member to make a purchase, but anyone can join by paying the $5 lifetime membership fee. The Barrie store is just off Highway 400 (exit 94, Essa Rd.).

Accommodations

Several chain motels cluster along Hart Drive (take the Dunlop St. exit from Hwy. 400), in an area that has nothing much to recommend it except views of the highway. Closer to downtown, you'll find B&Bs and small inns.

Owners Pam and Bob Richmond have set up a separate wing for guests on the second floor of their 1911 brick Georgian-style home east of downtown. The **Richmond Manor B&B** (16 Blake St., 705/726-7103, www.bbcanada.com, $80 s, $110 d) has two large, traditionally furnished guest rooms with peekaboo views of Kempenfelt Bay. A shared bath is located between the rooms, and across the hall is a guest lounge with a TV and DVD player. Breakfast is a formal affair, served on fine china in the stately dining room.

Catering to business travelers and people relocating to the Barrie area, the **Harbour View Inn** (1 Berczy St., 705/735-6832, www.harbourviewinn.ca, $129-349) has six rooms and suites—some with lake views—in a brick Victorian just east of downtown. While the accommodations aren't large, they all have kitchenettes, with a microwave, a mini fridge, a coffeemaker, a toaster, and dishes; some have sleep sofas to accommodate an extra guest.

Food

One of Ontario's largest and longest-running farmers markets, the year-round **Barrie Farmers Market** (Collier St. at Mulcaster St., www.barriefarmermarket.com, 8am-noon Sat.) has been operating since 1846. Selling seasonal produce, prepared foods, yummy baked goods, and crafts, the market is outside City Hall May to October; it moves inside City Hall from November to April.

Some of Barrie's most interesting food isn't downtown—it's in the strip malls and industrial parks off Highway 400. A good example is **Cravings Fine Food** (131 Commerce Park Dr., 705/734-2272, www.cravingsfinefood.ca, 9am-6pm Mon.-Tues., 9am-7pm Wed.-Fri., 9am-5pm Sat.), a café and gourmet shop that sells beautifully crafted (and scrumptious) pastries, sandwiches, salads, and other prepared foods, perfect for a quick meal on the road or to take north to the cottage.

If you love butter tarts, find your way to

the strip mall that houses **The Sweet Oven** (75 Barrie View Dr., Suite 103A, 705/733-9494, www.thesweetoven.com, 10am-6pm Mon.-Sat.), which makes these tasty tarts ($2, or $10 for six) in numerous varieties. Flavors like peanut butter, mint, or chai are novelties, but the classics—plain, pecan, or raisin—are the best.

Information and Services

You can pick up all sorts of information about Barrie and the surrounding region at the helpful **Tourism Barrie Visitor Information Centre** (205 Lakeshore Dr., 705/739-9444 or 800/668-9100, www.tourismbarrie.com, 9am-5pm Mon.-Fri., 10am-4pm Sat. Sept.-June, 9am-5pm Mon.-Fri., 10am-4pm Sat.-Sun. July-Aug.), located on the south side of Lake Simcoe. Tourism Barrie also staffs a seasonal **Downtown Information Kiosk** (Bayfield St. at Simcoe St., 9am-7pm daily May-mid-Oct.).

The provincially run **Ontario Travel Information Centre** (21 Mapleview Dr. E., 705/725-7280 or 800/567-1140, www.ontariotravel.net, 8am-8pm daily June-Aug., 8:30am-4:30pm daily Sept.-May), just off Highway 400, can help with travel questions about Barrie and points north.

Getting There and Around

From Toronto, both **Ontario Northland** (800/461-8558, www.ontarionorthland.ca, 90 minutes, adults $25 one-way) and **Greyhound** (800/661-8747, www.greyhound.ca, 90 minutes, adults $9-31 one-way) run frequent buses to the Barrie Bus Terminal (24 Maple Ave., 705/739-1500) downtown. Ontario Northland buses continue north from Barrie to Gravenhurst, Bracebridge, Huntsville, North Bay, Temagami, and Cochrane; another travels toward Parry Sound and Sudbury.

Simcoe County Airport Service (137 Brock St., 705/728-1148 or 800/461-7529, www.simcoecountyairportservice.ca, one-way $68 for 1 person, $96 for 2, $122 for 3,

$147 for 4) runs door-to-door van service from Toronto's Pearson Airport to Barrie.

Barrie Transit (705/739-4209, www.barrie.ca, $3), the city's bus service, can take you around town if you don't have a car. Get a transfer when you board, since it's good for 75 minutes, and parents, take note: up to three elementary school kids ride free with a paying adult.

Many car rental companies have Barrie offices, including **Avis** (www.avis.com), **Budget** (www.budget.ca), **Discount Car Rentals** (www.discountcar.com), and **Enterprise Rent-A-Car** (www.enterpriserentacar.ca).

ORILLIA

Though his day job was as a political science professor at Montreal's McGill University, Stephen Leacock (1869-1944) became famous as a writer and humorist. He published 35 humorous books, including *Sunshine Sketches of a Little Town* (1912) and *Arcadian Adventures of the Idle Rich* (1914).

In 1928, Leacock built a summer house near Old Brewery Bay in the town of Orillia. The home, which was his permanent residence following his retirement from McGill in 1936 until his death 12 years later, is now the **Stephen Leacock Museum** (50 Museum Dr., 705/329-1908, www.leacockmuseum.com, 10am-4pm daily June-Sept., 10am-4pm Mon.-Fri. Oct.-May, adults $5, seniors $4, students $3, kids $2). Some parts of the house are nearly as Leacock left them, including the sunroom with his worktable and his living room facing the lake. On the main floor are signed portraits of Leacock that noted photographer Yousuf Karsh took in 1941.

Orillia is 40 kilometers (25 miles) northeast of Barrie via Highway 11.

GRAVENHURST

You know you've arrived in Cottage Country when you pass by the **world's largest Muskoka chair** (1170 Muskoka Rd. S.), at the south end of town. What's a Muskoka chair, you ask? It's the laid-back wooden porch chair that most Americans call an Adirondack chair. This symbol of relaxation gives you a clue of what Gravenhurst is all about.

Gravenhurst's main attractions are at **Muskoka Wharf** (www.discovergravenhurst. com), the lakefront development where you can tour a boat museum or cruise the lake in a traditional steamship. The town is also the birthplace of Norman Bethune, a Canadian doctor who became wildly famous in China, where he's still considered a hero long after his death.

Gravenhurst Opera House (295 Muskoka Rd. S., 705/687-5550 or 888/495-8888, www.gravenhurstoperahouse.com), built in 1901, hosts concerts, plays, and films. **Music on the Barge** (Gull Lake Rotary Park, Brock St. at Bethune Dr., 7:30pm Sun. mid-June-mid-Aug.) has brought toe-tapping summer concerts, from big band to Dixieland to folk, to the waterfront since 1959.

★ Muskoka Wharf

The Muskoka Lakes Navigation Company opened in 1866, and during its heyday operated the largest fleet of inland lake steamships in North America. The ships carried passengers and freight across the Muskoka Lakes, providing service where the railroads didn't reach and roads either didn't go or were difficult to navigate. More than 100 lakeside hotels once operated in the Muskokas, and the guests all arrived by steamship.

One of these ships, the **RMS _Segwun,_** built in 1887 and used as an official Royal Mail Ship, remains North America's oldest operating steamship. **Muskoka Steamships** (185 Cherokee Lane, 705/687-6667 or 866/687-6667, www.realmuskoka.com, mid-June-mid-Oct., adults $21-50, kids $12.50-36) offers 1- to 4-hour sightseeing cruises on the _Segwun,_ departing from their Muskoka Wharf docks.

Back on land, explore the region's steamship traditions at the creatively designed **Muskoka Boat & Heritage Centre** (275 Steamship Bay Rd., 705/687-2115, www.realmuskoka.com, 10am-6pm Mon.-Fri., 10am-4pm Sat.-Sun. mid-June-mid-Oct., 10am-4pm Tues.-Sat. mid-Oct.-mid-June, adults $7.75, seniors $5.75, kids $3.75, families $18.75), filled with multimedia exhibits. In a recreated lakeside hotel, the owner welcomes you (in a video) and you can pretend that you're holidaying in the 19th century. Another exhibit is a recreated steamship that you can go aboard. Also visit the Grace and Speed Boathouse, North America's only in-water

Muskoka Boat & Heritage Centre in Gravenhurst

exhibit of working antique boats, with up to 20 spiffy craft on view. If you show your tickets from a Muskoka Steamships cruise, admission to the museum is free.

Bethune Memorial House National Historic Site

Gravenhurst-born surgeon Henry Norman Bethune (1890-1939) became a legendary physician, known largely for a brief tour of service on the other side of the world.

In 1938, after China and Japan went to war, Bethune traveled to China to tend to the injured, and after he arrived at the front, the legend of the foreign doctor's commitment to the Chinese began to spread. Bethune implemented a medical education program and established mobile medical facilities, including an operating theater that two mules could carry. After less than two years in the country, however, Bethune accidentally cut his finger while performing an operation, developed an aggressive form of blood poisoning, and died within the month. Chinese leader Mao Zedong wrote an essay, "In Memory of Norman Bethune," which became required reading for Chinese students and helped solidify Bethune's status as a hero in China.

The **Bethune Memorial House National Historic Site** (235 John St. N., 705/687-4261, www.pc.gc.ca, 10am-4pm daily July-mid.-Oct., 10am-4pm Wed.-Sun. June and mid-late Oct., adults $3.90, seniors $3.40, ages 6-16 $1.90, families $9.80) comprises two buildings: a modern museum that recounts Bethune's history, and the 1880 home where Bethune was born. Visit on a weekday if you can, when the house's diminutive rooms are less crowded and staff have more time to explain Bethune's legacy.

Tree Museum

One of Cottage Country's most offbeat attractions is this outdoor art gallery outside Gravenhurst. No, the **Tree Museum** (1634 Doe Lake Rd., 705/684-8185, www.thetree-museum.ca, dawn-dusk daily May-Oct., free)

isn't a museum of trees—it's a gallery outside in an 80-hectare (200-acre) woodland with imaginative sculptures and other eclectic works among the trees. Be prepared for lots of walking along the sometimes muddy paths. It's one kilometer (0.6 miles) from the parking area to the first sculpture, and another 1.2 kilometers (0.75 miles) to the center of the site; return the way you came. The museum has no restrooms or other facilities, so bring water and a snack.

To get to the Tree Museum, follow Highway 11 north past Gravenhurst, then exit at Doe Lake Road (Muskoka Rd. 6). Go east about eight kilometers (five miles) till you see museum signs on your right.

Accommodations

The **Residence Inn by Marriott** (285 Steamship Bay Rd., 705/687-6600 or 866/580-6238, www.marriott.com, $165-419 d) is located at Muskoka Wharf, overlooking Lake Muskoka. The 106 modern suites with kitchen facilities include studios with sleeper sofas and larger units with one or two bedrooms. Rates include buffet breakfast, parking, and Wi-Fi.

You won't be bored at **Taboo Resort** (1209 Muskoka Beach Rd., 705/687-2233 or 800/461-0236, www.tabooresort.com, mid-Feb.-Oct., $299-639 d), set in the woods on Lake Muskoka north of town. There's a private beach, four outdoor heated pools, golf, tennis, a spa, canoes, kayaks, and stand-up paddleboards, plus several restaurants and bars. The prime picks of the 101 guest rooms, done in sleek satiny woods, are right above the lake. Thirty individually decorated condos, with two to four bedrooms, are scattered around the property, although most don't have lake views.

Food

Though it looks a bit twee, with floral café curtains and blue-and-white china, the **Blue Willow Tea Shop** (900 Bay St., Muskoka Wharf, 705/687-2597, www.bluewillowtea-shop.ca, 11am-4pm Tues.-Thurs., 11am-8pm

Fri.-Sat., 11am-3pm Sun., $7-16) makes a good lakeside rest stop at Muskoka Wharf. They serve soups, salads, and sandwiches at lunch, along with a large selection of black, green, and fruit teas. Midafternoon, take a tea break with a scone or slice of cake, or settle in for traditional high tea ($23 pp).

You'll be fed well at the **Well Fed Deli** (150 Hotchkiss St., 705/684-9355, www.wellfedinc. com, 8am-3pm Mon., 8am-5pm Tues.-Fri., 10am-3pm Sat.), a diminutive downtown shop serving sandwiches (they roast their own turkey, beef, and peameal bacon), seasonal salads, and fresh-baked pastries. Most business is take-out, since there are just two sidewalk tables out front.

Information and Services
Muskoka Tourism (800/267-9700, www. discovermuskoka.ca) provides information about Gravenhurst and the rest of the Muskoka Lakes region. They operate a travel information center on Highway 11 south of Gravenhurst in the town of Kilworthy. Both the **Gravenhurst Chamber of Commerce** (www.gravenhurstchamber.com) and the **Town of Gravenhurst** (www.discovergravenhurst.com) provide visitor information online.

Getting There and Around
Gravenhurst is 180 kilometers (112 miles) north of Toronto and 75 kilometers (47 miles) north of Barrie. From Toronto, take Highway 400 north to Barrie, then continue north on Highway 11 into Gravenhurst.

From Toronto's Bay Street Station, **Ontario Northland** runs several daily buses to **Gravenhurst Station** (150 2nd St. S., 705/687-2301 or 800/461-8558, www.ontarionorthland.ca, 2.5-2.75 hours, one-way adults $41.20, seniors and students $35, ages 2-11 $20.55). **Northern Airport Shuttle** (705/474-7942 or 800/461-4219, www.northernairport.com, 2 hours, one-way adults $83) makes two scheduled trips a day in each direction between Toronto's Pearson Airport and Gravenhurst.

Exploring Gravenhurst is easiest if you have a car, although you can walk between Muskoka Wharf and the town center. The nearest car rental offices are in Bracebridge.

BRACEBRIDGE
Like many Muskoka towns, Bracebridge's tourism industry dates to the late 1800s, when visitors from Toronto arrived by train and boat. Most of the old-time resorts are gone, but the town's main street, Manitoba Street, has an old-timey feel that makes for a pleasant stroll. Bracebridge is a good base for exploring the region—it's an easy drive to Gravenhurst or Huntsville and to other towns along the surrounding lakes. With comfortable B&Bs and excellent restaurants, it's also a spot where you can just unwind.

Since the lakes are an important part of the Muskoka experience, get out on the water with **Lady Muskoka Cruises** (300 Ecclestone Dr., 705/646-2628 or 800/263-5239, www.ladymuskoka.com, noon Sat.-Sun. May-June, noon daily July-Aug., noon Sat.-Sun. and Wed. Sept.-mid-Oct., adults $29.20, seniors $27.43, students $22.12, ages 5-12 $14.60), which operates sightseeing boats on Lake Muskoka. Cruises depart at noon.

Bracebridge's own microbrewery, **Muskoka Brewery** (1964 Muskoka Beach Rd., 705/646-1266, www.muskokabrewery.com, 11am-5pm Mon.-Tues., 11am-6pm Wed.-Thurs., 11am-7pm Fri., 11am-5pm Sat., noon-4pm Sun. May-Oct., call for off-season hours), welcomes visitors to their shop. You can also tour the brewery (1:30pm, 2:30pm, and 3:30pm Thurs.-Sat.).

A Bracebridge summer tradition is the free **Bandshell Concert Series** (Memorial Park, Manitoba St., www.bracebridge.ca) on Thursday evenings from June through early September.

Accommodations
Sandy Yudin has run **Century House B&B** (155 Dill St., 705/645-9903, www.bbmuskoka.com/centuryhouse, $70-80 s, $80-100 d), the 1855 brick farmhouse she shares with

her husband, Norman Yan, for two decades, and knows how to make guests feel at home. The three traditional B&B rooms are furnished with quilts and wicker chairs and have all the essentials—comfortable beds, reading lamps, bathrobes—but no extraneous frills; they share two baths. Sandy's a great cook, serving multicourse breakfasts with fresh fruit, eggs, smoked trout, and toast with homemade marmalade. The B&B is a 15-minute walk to Manitoba Street's shops and restaurants.

Although it's just a short walk from the town center, the **Bay House Bed-and-Breakfast** (2 Dominion St., 705/645-7508, www.bbmuskoka.com/bayhouse, $128-168 d) feels like a cottage in the woods. The three lower-level guest rooms are done in cheery pastels. The largest has an electric fireplace and four-poster bed, while the Garden Room opens onto the patio. Jan and Peter Rickard are experienced innkeepers who are full of tips for things to do, although after their hearty breakfasts (which might include lemon ricotta pancakes or eggs hollandaise), you may be tempted just to soak in the outdoor hot tub.

Food

You can have a sandwich at **Marty's "World Famous" Café** (5 Manitoba St., 705/645-4794, www.martysworldfamous.com), but the shop's self-proclaimed fame is for the gooey caramel butter tarts. Just heed their advice not to eat these runny pastries in your car, or, as they warn, "You'll end up wearing them!"

A friendly joint for hanging out and sipping a microbrew, **The Griffin Gastropub** (9 Chancery Lane, 705/646-0438, www.thegriffinpub.ca, 4pm-midnight Wed., noon-2am Thurs.-Sat., $12-18) serves inventive pub grub, including addictive risotto balls, bison burgers, and sticky toffee pudding. Live folk, rock, blues, or jazz usually starts around 9pm Thursday through Saturday. The pub is at the top of a narrow alleyway, off Manitoba Street.

Don't be put off by the strip mall

setting; there's serious sushi savvy at the chic **Wabora Fusion Japanese Restaurant** (295 Wellington St. N., 705/646-9500, www.waborasushi.com, 11am-11pm daily, $8-20). The cavernous room has both an artfully arranged cocktail bar and a well-lit sushi bar where the chefs craft wildly imaginative *maki* rolls, like the Bracebridge (salmon, crab, asparagus, and gobo wrapped in cucumber with lemon-*ponzu*-caramel sauce) or the Spicy Cottage (shrimp tempura, crab, spicy tuna, greens, mango, and avocado in a rice paper roll). The straight-up *nigiri* are first-rate, too.

Colorful original artwork seems to pop from the walls at ★ **One Fifty Five** (155 Manitoba St., 705/645-1935, www.onefiftyfive.ca, lunch 11:30am-2:30pm Tues.-Sat., dinner 5pm-9:30pm Tues.-Sun., lunch $11-16, dinner $19-29), Bracebridge's white-tablecloth restaurant. The menu is colorful, too, with choices like crispy chicken *piccata* with grilled vegetable orzo or maple-cured rainbow trout. For dessert, it's hard to choose between the warm flourless chocolate cake and the lemon tart topped with fresh berries.

Information and Services

Tourism Bracebridge (1 Manitoba St., 705/645-8121 or 866/645-8121, www.tourismbracebridge.com) provides information about the area. Find more trip-planning details online at **The Heart of Muskoka** (www.theheartofmuskoka.com).

Getting There and Around

Bracebridge is 195 kilometers (121 miles) north of Toronto and 18 kilometers (11 miles) north of Gravenhurst. From Toronto, take Highway 400 north to Barrie, then continue north on Highway 11 to Bracebridge.

Ontario Northland (705/646-2239 or 800/461-8558, www.ontarionorthland.ca, 3 hours, one-way adults $44.50, seniors and students $37.75, ages 2-11 $22.20) buses from Toronto's Bay Street Station stop at the Riverside Inn (300 Ecclestone Dr.). Buses continue to Huntsville, North Bay, Temagami, and points farther north. **Northern Airport Shuttle** (705/474-7942 or 800/461-4219, www.northernairport.com, 2.25 hours, one-way adults $87) makes two scheduled trips a day in each direction between Toronto's Pearson Airport and Bracebridge.

Bracebridge is fairly compact and walk-able, but to explore the Muskoka region fur-ther, you need your own vehicle.

Huntsville and Vicinity

Located just west of Algonquin Provincial Park, the attractive town of Huntsville is a fa-vorite destination in its own right, with lots of outdoor activities, good places to eat, and a cute downtown. But it's also close enough to Algonquin that you can easily stay in town and make day trips into the park.

SIGHTS AND RECREATION

Start your Huntsville visit walking around downtown, looking for the **Group of Seven Outdoor Gallery** (www.groupofsevenoutdoorgallery.ca), more than 80 colorful wall murals that decorate town buildings. The murals are replicas of works by the Group of Seven artists who worked in Canada in the early 1900s.

Muskoka Heritage Place

If you're interested in the history of the Muskoka region, there's a lot to see at **Muskoka Heritage Place** (88 Brunel Rd., 705/789-7576, www.muskokaheritageplace. org, 10am-4pm daily mid-May-mid-Oct., last admission 3pm, adults $16.55, seniors $14.90, ages 3-12 $11.20). Your first stop should be in the **museum** (10am-4pm daily mid-May-mid-Oct., 10am-4pm Mon.-Fri. mid-Oct.-mid-May), which traces the region's roots from the early First Nations people, through the first European contact, the fur trading and lumber eras, and the evolution of the Muskokas as a tourist destination. More fun for kids is the **pioneer village** (mid-May-mid-Oct.), where wandering around the 20 restored buildings takes you back to the period between 1880 and 1910. Costumed interpreters demonstrate blacksmithing, woodworking, and other trades. You can ex-plore a trapper's cabin, a one-room school-house, and a First Nations encampment.

Catch a ride on the **Portage Flyer** steam train (100 Forbes Hill Dr., departs at noon, 1pm, 2pm, and 3pm Tues.-Sat. July-Aug., check the website for off-season schedule, adults $5.70, seniors $5.10, ages 3-12 $3.50), which ran from 1904 to 1959 in nearby Dwight along the world's smallest commercial railroad. It operated on a 1.8-kilometer-long (1.125-mile) narrow-gauge track as a portage, ferrying supplies and travelers across a sliver of land between Peninsula Lake and Portage Bay. The train trip runs about 30 minutes and includes a stop at the **Rail Museum,** a re-creation of a 1920s train station, where you can learn more about the role of railroads and steamboats in the Muskokas' development. If you're a train enthusiast, note that the steam engine pulls the train only in July and August; in spring and fall, a diesel locomotive does the work, to help preserve the steam engine's life.

Muskoka Heritage Place is just a few min-utes' drive from downtown Huntsville. From Main Street, go south on Brunel Road. The train depot is a short distance from the main entrance; watch for the signs.

Arrowhead Provincial Park

Through far smaller and less well known than nearby Algonquin, the four-sea-son **Arrowhead Provincial Park** (451 Arrowhead Park Rd., 705/789-5105, www. ontarioparks.com/park/arrowhead, $14.50 per vehicle), on Arrowhead Lake 10 kilo-meters (six miles) north of Huntsville, is a

Huntsville

To North Bay and
Arrowhead Provincial Park

To Algonquin
Provincial Park

11

60

HANES RD

KING WILLIAM ST

WEST RD

WEST RD

CONGDEN ST N

HUNTSVILLE ■
BUS STATION

RODEWAY INN
● KING WILLIAM

THAT LITTLE PLACE
BY THE LIGHTS

ALGONQUIN
OUTFITTERS

MAIN ST E

Fairy
Lake

CHAMBER OF ■
COMMERCE

ALGONQUIN
THEATRE

★

WEST ST S

Hunters

Bay

SPENCER'S
TALL TREES

▼

BRUNEL RD

MUSKOKA
HERITAGE
PLACE
★

WEST SIDE FISH
AND CHIPS ▼

FLORENCE ST W

11

MAIN ST W

YONGE ST

TOWN LINE RD W

0   0.5 mi
0   0.5 km

To Barrie

© AVALON TRAVEL

family-friendly outdoor destination with lots to do year-round. If you purchase a day-use pass at either Arrowhead or Algonquin, you can use that pass in both parks.

For day **hiking,** Arrowhead has 15 kilometers (nine miles) of easy-to-moderate trails, including the 5.3-kilometer (3.3-mile) Arrowhead Lake Trail that circles the lakeshore. A short walk from the parking lot on Roe Campground Road leads to the **Big Bend Lookout,** which overlooks the winding Big East River. Arrowhead Lake has several **swimming** beaches, and the waters here and on smaller Mayflower Lake are calm spots for **paddling.** You can rent canoes, kayaks, stand-up paddleboards, and bicycles (including fat-tire trail bikes) at the Beach Information Building in July-August and from the main park office in the spring and fall. In winter, Arrowhead's hiking paths become cross-country ski trails; ski rentals are available. The park also floods a road to create a groomed 1.3-kilometer (0.8-mile) **ice-skating trail** through the woods.

Limberlost Forest and Wildlife Reserve

An excellent, less-visited hiking destination is the privately owned **Limberlost Forest and Wildlife Reserve** (S. Limberlost Rd., 705/635-1584, www.limberlostlodges.com, 9am-5pm daily, free), where more than 70 kilometers (44 miles) of trails circle many of the property's 20 lakes as they crisscross the forested 4,045-hectare (10,000-acre) reserve. Check the website or ask at the reserve office for the extremely detailed *Master Trail Guide,* which tells you about each of the trails and their notable features; it also includes trail maps.

From Huntsville, follow Highway 60 east for about 10 kilometers (six miles), then turn left (north) onto Limberlost Road (Muskoka Rd. 8). Continue another nine kilometers (5.6

miles), and turn right onto South Limberlost Road and follow it for three kilometers (1.8 miles) to the reserve entrance. The gates of the reserve look imposing, but pull up and they'll slide open.

Treetop Trekking

In a wooded park east of Huntsville, this adventure company (1180 Hwy. 60, 705/788-9000 or 855/788-9009, www.treetoptrekking.com, mid-Mar.-Oct., adults $64, ages 12-15 $54, ages 9-11 $47) offers three-hour outdoor experiences that include up to seven **zip lines** and multiple **aerial ropes courses** ranging 3 to 21 meters (10 to 70 feet) high. A highlight (or terror-inducer) is the Tarzan jump, a controlled leap from a platform high in the trees. Phone for reservations, which are required; they'll try to accommodate same-day requests. Kids under age 16 must be accompanied by an adult, and the website details age, height, and weight requirements. Ask about family discounts.

ENTERTAINMENT AND SHOPPING

The **Algonquin Theatre** (37 Main St. E., 705/789-4975 or 877/989-4975, www.algonquintheatre.ca) stages concerts, plays, and lectures, featuring performers from near and far. The **Huntsville Festival of the Arts** (705/789-4975, www.huntsvillefestival. on.ca) brings concerts, art workshops, and other events to venues around town; many are outdoors and free. For ticketed events, buy tickets online, by phone, or in person at the Algonquin Theatre.

Shops along Huntsville's Main Street sell outdoor gear, artwork, and souvenirs. **Algonquin Outfitters Huntsville** (86 Main St. E., 705/787-0262 or 800/469-4948, www.algonquinoutfitters.com, 9:30am-6pm Mon.-Wed., 9:30am-8pm Thurs.-Fri., 9am-6pm Sat., 11am-4pm Sun. July-early Sept., 10am-6pm Mon.-Fri., 9am-5pm Sat., 11am-4pm Sun. early Sept.-June) stocks outdoor clothing and camping supplies and rents canoes, kayaks, and bikes.

They also have a store closer to Algonquin Park, **Algonquin Outfitters Oxtongue Lake** (1035 Algonquin Outfitters Rd., Dwight, 705/635-2243 or 800/469-4948, www.algonquinoutfitters.com, 8am-6pm Mon.-Thurs., 8am-7pm Fri.-Sun. July-early Sept., 9am-5pm Mon.-Thurs., 8am-6pm Fri.-Sat., 9am-6pm Sun. May-June and early Sept.-mid-Oct., 9am-5pm daily mid-Oct.-Apr.) that has canoe, kayak, and bike rentals. They offer

paddling at Arrowhead Provincial Park

guided canoe and kayak trips in and around Algonquin Park, too.

ACCOMMODATIONS

Lodgings in and around Huntsville range from basic in-town motels to B&Bs hidden in the woods, cottage colonies, and upscale resorts. Many accommodations are off Highway 60 east of town. Closer to Algonquin's West Gate, in the tiny town of Dwight, more lodgings cluster around Oxtongue Lake.

Huntsville

The 32-unit **Rodeway Inn King William** (23 King William St., 705/789-9661 or 888/995 9169, www.kingwilliaminn.com, $129-189 d) is the nicest of the in-town motels, upgraded with crisp white linens, newer furnishings, and mini fridges. The standard rooms, with either two doubles or one double and one queen, are slightly smaller but otherwise similar to the queen rooms, which have one queen and a sleep sofa. The largest rooms are kings with a whirlpool tub. Wi-Fi is included.

East of Huntsville

A stay at **The Morgan House** (83 Morgans Rd., 705/380-2566 or 866/311-1727, www.morganhousewoolworks.ca, $100-110 d), a bed-and-breakfast in a comfortable stone country home, is like a holiday with good friends on their mostly organic farm. Co-owner Pam Carnochan, a wool artist, welcomes guests on the screened-in porch or in the parlor with its overstuffed furniture. Upstairs, the two simple guest rooms, with traditional quilts on the beds, share one large bath. Breakfast includes homemade baked goods and eggs from the farm's hens. Families are welcome.

A suburban home set amid gardens, and, yes, tranquil woods, the **Tranquil Woods Victorian Inn** (50 North Portage Rd., 705/788-7235, www.tranquilwoods.ca, $130-145 d) is Victorian in style, but it's in a newly built house with high ceilings and an airy feel. Personable owners Judy and Dan offer touring tips while serving a hearty breakfast. The largest of the three guest rooms is on the main floor, with a private patio. Upstairs,

the Red Oak room has a sleigh bed and Victorian furnishings, while the red-walled Scarlett Maple room is more country cottage.

Over breakfast at the ★ **Pow-Wow Point Lodge** (207 Grassmere Resort Rd., 705/789-4951 or 800/461-4263, www.powwowpointlodge.com, $290-450 pp for 2 nights), staff ring a bell and announce the day's activities, such as sandcastle contests and swimming races, just like at summer camp. There's a lakeside beach for swimming and canoeing, tennis courts, and shuffleboard. Accommodations include basic lodge rooms and cottages and more updated units, but all feel homey. Owners Doug and Dee Howell have run the lodge since 1989, and many guests return year after year. Rates include three ample meals; rates for kids and teens are discounted.

You won't be bored at the classy **Deerhurst Resort** (1235 Deerhurst Dr., 705/789-6411 or 800/461-4393, www.deerhurstresort.com, $239-719 d, resort fee $25 per room), with activities such as golf, tennis, trail rides, and zip-lining. The lake has water slides, trampolines, and all kinds of watersports. In winter, there's cross-country skiing and ice-skating. Accommodations include standard hotel rooms and 1- to 3-bedroom condos with full kitchens. The main dining room, serves contemporary fare with local ingredients; several more casual eateries are scattered around the property. A high-energy musical show, performed several nights a week in summer and fall, is great fun.

Dwight and Oxtongue Lake

The cheapest beds near Algonquin are at the laid-back **Wolf Den Hostel and Nature Retreat** (4568 Hwy. 60, Oxtongue Lake, 705/635-9336 or 866/271-9336, www.wolfdenbunkhouse.com, year-round, $27 dorm, $45-85 s, $68-85 d, $90-125 cabins). Located between Dwight and the West Gate, the property's main lodge has a shared kitchen, a large lounge, and guest rooms. Two log bunkhouses have an eight-bed dorm upstairs and rooms for four to five on the main level. Baths are central and shared. There's no meal service, so bring your own provisions.

A small cluster of lodgings sits along Oxtongue Lake, just off Highway 60, about a 10-minute drive from Algonquin's West Gate. It's a pretty setting, although the proximity of Highway 60 and its traffic noise can be bothersome. Under the same ownership as the Bartlett Lodge in Algonquin Park, **The Pines Cottage Resort** (1032 Oxtongue Lake Rd., Dwight, 705/635-2379, www.algonquinparkaccommodations.com, mid-May-mid-Oct., $170-250) has family-friendly one- and two-bedroom cottages with fully equipped kitchens in the woods above Oxtongue Lake, where there's a sandy beach. Rates include the use of canoes and kayaks.

More modern, but a little closer to Highway 60, the year-round **Blue Spruce Resort** (4308 Hwy. 60, Dwight, 705/635-2330, www.bluespruce.ca, $142-339) has both hotel-style suites and stand-alone 1- to 3-bedroom cottages, all with kitchens. There are tennis courts, a swimming beach, coin-operated laundry, and Wi-Fi.

Camping

Arrowhead Provincial Park (451 Arrowhead Park Rd., 705/789-5105, www.ontarioparks.com, mid-May-mid-Oct., tent sites $40, electrical sites $46) has three campgrounds with a total of 378 campsites, 185 with electrical service. The Roe Campground is the most secluded, and the forested Lumbly Campground—with no electrical sites—is closest to the lakes and feels the most rustic. The large East River Campground accommodates RVs and also has five camping cabins ($142); the cabins are heated and sleep up to five. The campgrounds all have central flush toilets and showers.

FOOD
Huntsville

Two of the best spots for picnic supplies or a meal to go are located on Highway 60, just east of town, and both have similar names. The **Farmer's Daughter** (118 Hwy. 60, 705/789-5700, www.fresheverything.ca, 8am-6pm Mon.-Wed., 8am-7pm Thurs.-Fri., 8am-6pm Sat., 8am-5pm Sun.) is a combination prepared food counter, bakery, and gourmet market. They sell fresh produce, sandwiches made to order, and fancy fixings like smoked fish pâté and homemade jams. Their baked goods, including the addictive trail mix bars, are excellent.

Across the road, the **Butcher's Daughters** (133 Hwy. 60, 705/789-2848, www.butchersdaughters.ca, 9am-6pm Mon.-Sat., 10am-4pm Sun. July-Aug., 9am-6pm Mon.-Sat. June and Sept., 9am-6pm Tues.-Sat. Oct.-May, $4.50-8) makes good deli sandwiches, interesting soups, and salads. There's a small seating area, or you can take your food to go.

For many Ontarians, a trip to Cottage Country isn't complete without a stop at the old-style, family-friendly **West Side Fish and Chips** (126 Main St. W., 705/789-7200, www.westsidefishandchips.com, 8am-8pm daily, $5-17) for a hearty plate of halibut and chips and a gooey slice of coconut cream pie. They're always busy, but you can amuse yourself with trivia game cards while you wait.

You know **That Little Place by the Lights** (76 Main St. E., 705/789-2536, www.thatlittleplacebythelights.ca, 9am-9pm Mon.-Sat., 11am-4pm Sun., lunch $5-14, dinner $12-15)? It's a cozy Italian trattoria masquerading as a touristy ice cream parlor and coffee shop. The sauces for the pastas and pizzas are homemade (try the spicy linguini puttanesca with olives, capers, anchovies, and peppers), and the salads are simple but fresh. It's family friendly, too, especially if you promise the kids gelato for dessert.

The long-running **Spencer's Tall Trees** (87 Main St. W., 705/789-9769, www.spencerstalltrees.com, 5pm-close Mon., 11:30am-2pm and 5pm-close Tues.-Fri., 5pm-close Sat., call for seasonal hours, lunch $11-21, dinner $18-49) is set in a heritage house amid, yes, tall trees. In the several dining nooks, you can sup on classics like venison with spaetzle, veal Oscar (topped with crab), or pickerel in a maple-thyme-butter sauce. Lunch options range from salads and sandwiches to pastas. To finish with something sweet, try the chocolate pâté or a seasonal fruit crumble.

Dwight and Oxtongue Lake
The perpetual lines attest to the popularity of **Henrietta's Pine Bakery** (2868 Hwy. 60, Dwight, 705/635-2214, www.henriettaspine-bakery.net, 9am-5pm Mon.-Sat., 10am-4pm Sun. May-mid-Oct.), where specialties include sticky buns and a highly recommended scone-like cranberry pastry called the Muskoka cloud. Come early in the day, since they close when the goodies sell out.

INFORMATION AND SERVICES
The **Huntsville/Lake of Bays Chamber of Commerce** (8 West St. N., 705/789-4771, www.huntsvilleadventures.com), just off Main Street, can provide more information about events and things to do in the Huntsville-Algonquin region.

GETTING THERE
Car
Huntsville is 215 kilometers (133 miles) north of Toronto and 35 kilometers (22 miles) north of Bracebridge. From Toronto, take Highway 400 north to Barrie, then continue north on Highway 11 to Huntsville.

Bus
Ontario Northland (705/789-6431 or 800/461-8558, www.ontarionorthland.ca, 3.75-4 hours, one-way adults $54.50, seniors and students $46.25, ages 2-11 $27.25) operates buses from the Toronto Central Bus Station to **Huntsville Bus Depot** (77 Centre St. N.), which is one kilometer (0.6 miles) north of Main Street. Buses continue from Huntsville to North Bay, Temagami, Cochrane, and other northern destinations.

To get to Huntsville directly from Toronto's Pearson airport, you can take the **Northern Airport Shuttle** (705/474-7942 or 800/461-4219, www.northernairport.com, 2.75 hours, one-way adults $91), which runs two daily trips in each direction.

GETTING AROUND
While it's easy to get to Huntsville without a car, exploring the region around town, including Algonquin Park, is difficult without your own wheels. If you don't have your own car, you can take the bus to Huntsville, then rent a car to explore Algonquin. **Enterprise Rent-A-Car** (174 Main St. W., 705/789-1834 or 800/736-8222, www.enterpriserentacar.ca) and **Discount Car Rentals** (8 Ott Dr., 705/788-3737, www.discountcar.com) have Huntsville locations.

Algonquin Provincial Park

If you visit only one of Ontario's many outdoor destinations, the province's first provincial park is an excellent choice. Measuring 763,000 hectares (1.9 million acres), immense **Algonquin Provincial Park** (705/633-5572, www.ontarioparks.com or www.algonquin-park.on.ca) stretches across a wide swath of Northeastern Ontario. Covered with hardwood and coniferous forests, the region was a major logging area in the 1800s, and many visitors are surprised to learn that limited logging is still allowed in the park. When the park was created in 1893, it wasn't to bring a halt to logging, but rather to protect the region's wildlife. The park's earliest tourists arrived by train, disembarking at a rail depot near Cache Lake and staying in a nearby hotel. In the 1930s, Highway 60 was built across Algonquin's southern sections, and as more tourists came by road, rail service was discontinued. The prevailing wisdom was that eliminating train service would keep the park more "natural."

Highway 60 is still the main access route for visitors entering the West Gate from Huntsville (or Toronto) or the East Gate from Ottawa. If your time is limited, pick a few stops—perhaps a paddle at Canoe Lake, hiking one or two of the shorter trails—and spend an hour at the exhibits in the park Visitors Centre. Despite the park's popularity, you can find quiet trails and canoe routes to explore even if you stay near Highway 60. But Algonquin offers ample opportunities to get out into the wilderness, too; most of the park's vast backcountry is reachable only by canoe. Algonquin Park is open year-round, although many park services and sights operate only from April or May until mid-October.

SIGHTS

The park's main sights are listed from west to east along Highway 60, the direction you'll reach them coming from Toronto or elsewhere in the Muskokas. Distances are from the park's West Gate, so a sight at "Km. 20" is 20 kilometers east of the West Gate. From Ottawa, Peterborough, and the Kawarthas, or from elsewhere in Eastern Ontario, enter the park from the East Gate (at Km. 56) and follow these locations in reverse.

West Gate (Hwy. 60, Km. 0)

At Algonquin's western entrance, staff can help you get oriented and provide information about things to do, particularly helpful if your time is limited. All visitors must purchase a park permit ($17 per vehicle) and display it on the dashboard. Permits are available at the East and West Gates and at the Algonquin Park Visitors Centre. If you're driving across the park on Highway 60 without stopping, you don't need a permit; but if you stop anywhere in the park, even to use a restroom, you must have a permit or risk being fined.

If you're spending several days in the park or visiting multiple parks, consider purchasing an **Ontario Parks seasonal pass,** which allows unlimited day visits to any Ontario provincial parks. You can buy a summer-only pass (valid Apr.-Nov., $107.50), a winter-only pass (Dec.-Mar., $70), or a full-year pass (Apr.-Mar., $150.50).

Canoe Lake (Hwy. 60, Km. 14.1)

The history of Canoe Lake is inextricably linked to the mysterious disappearance of the painter Tom Thomson (1877-1917), a member of the Group of Seven artists who lived and worked in Ontario in the early 1900s. Beginning in 1912, Thomson spent several

You can kayak or canoe on Algonquin's Canoe Lake.

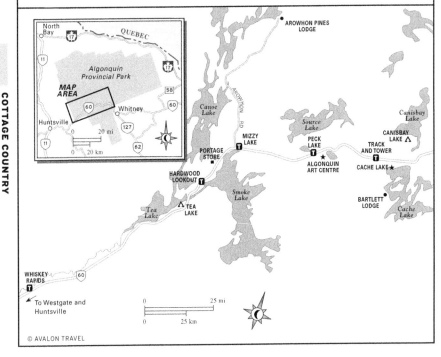

Algonquin Provincial Park

years painting in Algonquin Park, mostly on and around Canoe Lake. Thomson was last seen on July 8, 1917, in the vicinity of Canoe Lake—and then he vanished. His overturned canoe was found behind the lake's Wapomeo Island, and several days later, his body was pulled from the lake. The exact circumstances of his death remain a puzzle that has never been solved. In his memory, the **Tom Thomson memorial cairn** was erected in 1930 on one of Thomson's favorite Canoe Lake campsites. The cairn is accessible only by canoe.

The **Portage Store** (Hwy. 60, Km. 14.1, 705/633-5622, www.portagestore.com, late Apr.-mid-Oct.) on Canoe Lake rents canoes and can give you tips on where to go, including how to get to the Thomson cairn. They also offer half-day and full-day guided paddles.

Algonquin Art Centre (Hwy. 60, Km. 20)

The **Algonquin Art Centre** (705/633-5555, www.algonquinartcentre.com, 10am-5pm daily June-mid-Oct.) has a small gallery (donation) that shows changing exhibits of works by artists who have an Algonquin connection. The center also offers drop-in art activities (10:30am-4:30pm daily July-Aug., $10-25) for both children and adults.

Cache Lake (Hwy. 60, Km. 23.5)

Cache Lake was once the center of activity in Algonquin Park. From the 1890s, when the park was first established, until the 1950s, this lake area had a rail depot—Algonquin Park Station—as well as a large hotel. All that remains today, aside from the lovely lake itself, is a short historical walking trail, where several

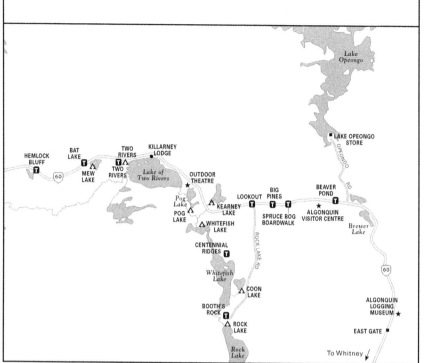

signs with historical photos along a wooded path tell you about the area's interesting past.

Lake of Two Rivers
(Hwy. 60, Km. 31)

Lake of Two Rivers is a busy place. In addition to the large **Two Rivers Campground** (705/633-5572), there's a snack bar, a grocery store, and mountain bike rentals. East of the campground, **Killarney Lodge** (Lake of Two Rivers, Hwy. 60, Km. 33.2, 705/633-5551 or 877/767-5935, www.killarneylodge.com) is set on the Lake of Two Rivers. Just east of the lodge is a public swimming beach.

Algonquin Visitors Centre
(Hwy. 60, Km. 43)

Even if you've entered the park from the west, it's worth stopping into the **Algonquin Visitors Centre** (9am-5pm daily late Apr.-Oct., 9am-4pm Mon.-Fri., 9am-5pm Sat.-Sun. Nov.-late Apr., daily hours during holiday weeks) to learn more about the park. Start by watching a 12-minute film about the park's history and natural features, then visit the exhibit area, which covers these topics in more detail. In summer, many interpretive programs are based at the Visitors Centre. A shop sells detailed park maps and guides as well as books about wildlife, camping, and the outdoors. There's a basic cafeteria (springfall), and free Wi-Fi.

What's the best feature of the Visitors Centre? It's the deck out back, which overlooks a wide swath of park territory and helps you appreciate Algonquin's expanse. There's another overlook from the short **Fire Tower Trail,** a boardwalk that leads to a reconstructed cupola, the lookout at the top of a fire tower.

Howling with the Wolves

One of the many animals that live in the Algonquin Provincial Park wilderness is the wolf. And one of the most popular (and eeriest) activities at Algonquin Park is the Wolf Howl. These events typically attract more than 1,500 visitors, who assemble at the park's Outdoor Theatre (Hwy. 60, Km. 35.4) for a presentation about wolves and their habitat. Then everyone gets in their cars and drives caravan-style to a designated spot where park naturalists have heard a wolf pack on the previous night. Once everyone is in place, the naturalists begin a sequence of howls—hoping that the wolves will respond with howls of their own. Sometimes they do, and sometimes they don't, but if you're lucky enough to hear the wolf pack howling, it's a unique experience.

The Wolf Howls are typically held during August, occasionally the first week of September, the only time of year when wolves are likely to remain in one place for days at a time. The howls are held once a week, at 8pm Thursday, and last about three hours. Check event bulletin boards throughout the park, or phone the **Visitors Centre** (613/637-2828) to confirm if the week's Wolf Howl will be held. Howls are canceled if no wolves are in an area along Highway 60 or if the weather is inclement, so you generally won't know till the day of the event whether it will take place. Updates on the Wolf Howls are also posted on the **Friends of Algonquin Park website** (www.algonquinpark.on.ca), where you can sign up to receive an email update on the week's Wolf Howl.

Algonquin Logging Museum (Hwy. 60, Km. 54.5)

Logging was an important part of Algonquin's heritage. Learn more about that history and about the delicate balance between industry and preservation at the **Algonquin Logging Museum** (9am-5pm daily late June-mid-Oct., free). You can watch a short video about Algonquin's logging history, but the most interesting parts of this museum are outdoors.

As you follow a walking trail through a recreated logging camp, you can see how loggers cut and squared the trees, hauled them across the lakes, and drove them through water chutes to transport them to the cities. You can climb aboard an "alligator," a steam-powered tugboat used to haul logs. The trail also takes you past a working log dam and chute, a restored blacksmith shop, a locomotive, and a classic 1950s truck. There are enough things to touch and climb on that kids may enjoy it, even if they don't appreciate the historical angle.

East Gate (Hwy. 60, Km. 55.8)

Like the West Gate, Algonquin's eastern entrance has an information office that sells the required park permits ($17 per vehicle), provides park maps, and offers suggestions about things to see and do. If you're driving east toward Ottawa, you can use the restrooms here before hitting the road.

SPORTS AND RECREATION
Bicycling

Algonquin Park has two cycling trails that are easy to reach from Highway 60. The relatively flat, family-friendly 16-kilometer (10-mile) **Old Railway Bike Trail** follows the route of a former rail line between Cache Lake and the Rock Lake Campground. The trail passes the campgrounds at Mew Lake, Lake of Two Rivers, Kearney Lake, Pog Lake, Whitefish Lake, and Coon Lake. The more challenging **Minnesing Mountain Bike Trail** (Hwy. 60, Km. 23, late-June-mid-Oct.) includes four hilly loops of 4.7, 10.1, 17.1, and 23.4 kilometers (2.9, 6.3, 10.6, and 14.5 miles). The trail is often quite muddy in June and July.

You can rent bikes at the **Two Rivers Store** (Hwy. 60, Km. 31.4, 705/633-5622) and the **Opeongo Store** (Lake Opeongo, 6.2 km/3.9 miles north of Km. 46.3, 613/637-2075 or 888/280-8886, www.algonquinoutfitters.com).

★ Canoeing

Algonquin Park is one of Ontario's most popular destinations for canoeing. Not only can you paddle on the park's numerous lakes and rivers, but Algonquin also has more than 2,000 kilometers (1,240 miles) of canoe routes across the backcountry, ideal for overnight or multiday canoe trips. A useful planning resource is the **Canoe Routes of Algonquin Provincial Park Map** (www.algongquin-park.on.ca, $5), which you can order online or purchase at any of the park stores or information centers. It details all the lakes, access points, portages, and campsites across Algonquin.

Within the park, you can rent canoes at the **Portage Store** (Canoe Lake, Hwy. 60, Km. 14.1, www.portagestore.com) and the Opeongo Store (6.2 km/3.9 miles north of Km. 46.3), run by **Algonquin Outfitters** (613/637-2075 or 888/280-8886, www.algon-quinoutfitters.com). Both outfitters offer shuttle services to take you and your canoe to various launch points. Many outfitters outside the park will rent canoes with car-top carriers.

Both the Portage Store and Algonquin Outfitters offer guided canoe day trips. The Portage Store runs a full-day trip (9:30am-4:30pm daily late June-early Sept., 9:30am-4:30pm Tues., Thurs., and Sat.-Sun. mid-May-late June and early Sept.-early Oct., adults $60, under age 14 $30) on Canoe Lake, which includes an orientation about the park, basic canoe instruction, and a day-long paddle with a stop for a picnic lunch. In July and August they also offer a half-day trip (1pm-5pm, adults $36, under age 14 $18). Reservations are advised for both trips.

From their Opeongo Store, Algonquin Outfitters offers a guided half-day Costello Creek trip (Mon.-Fri. mid-May-Oct., $70 pp for 2 people, $47 pp for 3, $35 pp for 4). They also run a full-day guided canoe trip (9am Mon.-Fri. mid-May-Oct., $150 pp for 2, $100 pp for 3, $75 pp for 4) departing from their Oxtongue Lake store. Reservations are required for all trips. Ask about discounts for kids and teens.

Hiking

All along the Highway 60 corridor are trails for day hikes, ranging from an easy boardwalk path to strenuous all-day excursions. More experienced hikers can tromp along more than 140 kilometers (87 miles) of backpacking trails through the park's interior.

The most accessible park trails:

· **Whiskey Rapids** (Km. 7.2, 2.1 km/1.3 miles, moderate)

· **Hardwood Lookout** (Km. 13.8, 0.8 km/0.5 miles, moderate)

· **Mizzy Lake** (Km. 15.4, 11 km/7 miles, moderate)

· **Peck Lake** (Km. 19.2, 1.9 km/1.2 miles, moderate)

· **Track and Tower** (Km. 25, 7.7 km/4.8 miles, moderate)

· **Hemlock Bluff** (Km. 27.2, 3.5 km/2.2 miles, moderate)

· **Bat Lake** (Km. 30, 5.6 km/3.5 miles, moderate)

· **Two Rivers** (Km. 31, 2.1 km/1.3 miles, moderate)

· **Centennial Ridges** (Km. 37.6, 10 km/6 miles, strenuous)

· **Lookout** (Km. 39.7, 1.9 km/1.2 miles, moderate)

· **Big Pines** (Km. 40.3, 2.9 km/1.8 miles, moderate)

· **Booth's Rock** (Km. 40.5, 5.1 km/3.2 miles, moderate)

· **Spruce Bog Boardwalk** (Km. 42.5, 1.5 km/0.9 miles, easy)

· **Beaver Pond** (Km. 45.2, 2 km/1.2 miles, moderate)

Trail guides, with more details about each of these hikes, are available at the trailheads (spring to fall) and online (www.algonquin-park.on.ca).

Winter Sports

If you want to try dogsledding, these outfitters can get you out on the Algonquin trails. **Voyageur Quest** (416/486-3605 or 800/794-9660, www.voyageurquest.com) offers one-day, weekend-long and multiday dogsledding trips (Dec.-Mar., weather permitting). **Snow Forest Adventures** (705/783-0461, www.snowforestadventures.ca, late Dec.-Mar.) runs half-day (adults $150 pp) and full-day ($250 pp) dogsledding trips that depart from the Sunday Lake dogsledding trails (Hwy. 60, Km. 40). No experience is necessary, and kids under 12 can ride with a paying adult for $50 (half-day) and $100 (full-day).

Algonquin Park has three areas that offer trails for cross-country skiing. At the West Gate, the groomed **Fen Lake Ski Trail** has four loops, ranging 1.25-13 kilometers (0.75-8 miles). One kilometer (0.6 miles) west of the East Gate, the groomed **Leaf Lake Trail** has routes measuring 5 to 51 kilometers (3-32 miles) in length. For more challenging wilderness skiing, head to the **Minnesing Trail** (Hwy. 60, Km. 23), where four ungroomed loops range 4.7 to 23.4 kilometers (3-14.5 miles). For snowshoeing, you can explore nearly anywhere in the park, including any of the hiking trails along Highway 60. Snowshoes are not allowed on the cross-country trails.

In winter, you still need to purchase a park permit ($17 per vehicle). Also make sure you have ample time to get off the trails before dark, and wear warm clothes, particularly hats, gloves, boots, and multiple layers appropriate for your outdoor activity.

Outfitters

A number of outfitters, both within and outside Algonquin Park, can help you organize canoeing, camping, and hiking trips; rent you the gear you need; or take you on a guided journey. Some even organize dogsledding excursions. **Algonquin Outfitters** (800/469-4948, www.algonquinoutfitters.com) has locations throughout the Muskoka region, including the Opeongo Store on Lake Opeongo within the park, Oxtongue Lake outside the West Gate, and Huntsville. They offer a

variety of guided or self-guided trips, including half-day, full-day, and multiday canoe and kayak excursions. Located on Canoe Lake, the **Portage Store** (Hwy. 60, Km. 14.1, 705/633-5622, www.portagestore.com, late Apr.-mid-Oct.) organizes canoe trips and offers half-, full-, and multiday guided paddles. Outside the East Gate, **Opeongo Outfitters** (29902 Hwy. 60, Whitney, 613/637-5470 or 800/790-1864, www.opeongooutfitters.com, mid-Apr.-mid-Oct.) can rent gear for a multiday canoe trip, including a canoe, tent, a pack, a sleeping bag, food, cooking utensils, and other supplies. You can also rent a kayak or canoe for the day.

Voyageur Quest (416/486-3605 or 800/794-9660, www.voyageurquest.com) organizes several different Algonquin excursions, such as three- to seven-day canoe trips (including trips designed for families), a moose photography safari, and winter dogsledding trips. **Northern Edge Algonquin** (888/383-8320, www.northernedgealgonquin.com) runs a stand-up paddling safari and yoga retreat; a weekend of hiking, canoeing, and wildlife spotting; and a multiday canoe adventure across Algonquin's remote backcountry. Run by the Algonquin First Nation of Wolf Lake, **Algonquin Canoe Company** (705/981-0572 or 866/889-9788, www.algonquincanoe.com) offers guided daylong and multiday canoe trips as well as cultural tours, including a weekend of traditional drumbuilding and drumming. **Snow Forest Adventures** (705/783-0461, www.snowforestadventures.ca) offers half-day and full-day dogsledding trips, from late December through March, weather permitting.

ACCOMMODATIONS AND FOOD

If you want to stay within the park, you can choose from three upscale lodges (which also operate restaurants), rustic former ranger cabins, yurts, or camping. The lodges, cabins, and most of the campgrounds are open spring to fall. In winter, you can camp at Mew Lake, off Highway 60, or out in the backcountry. The park cafeterias and snack bars also operate seasonally.

Park Lodges

With hiking, swimming and canoeing, there's plenty to do at **Arowhon Pines** (Arowhon Rd., 705/633-5661 or 866/633-5661, www.arowhonpines.ca, late May-mid-Oct., $205-450 pp). The private cabins have a queen bed, lounge area, and private deck. The less-expensive shared cabins have a private room and bath, but share the lounge space with guests. Lodging rates include breakfast, lunch, and dinner as well as use of all the recreational facilities. To reach Arowhon Pines, follow Highway 60 to Km. 16, then turn north onto Arowhon Rd., which winds through the woods to the lodge.

Getting to **Bartlett Lodge** (Cache Lake, 705/633-5543 or 866/614-5355, www.bartlett-lodge.com, mid-May-late Oct.) is half the fun; the lodge is accessible only by boat. When you turn off Highway 60 at Km. 23.5, call the lodge, which will send their water taxi. Some of the lakeside one- to three-bedroom cabins ($179-265 pp) date to the early 1900s. Studio units ($165-199 pp) are in a historic log cabin. Rates include buffet breakfast and a multicourse dinner. The lodge also offers a "glamorous camping" option in a furnished **platform tent** ($105-135 pp, including breakfast); a washroom with showers is in an adjacent building.

Killarney Lodge (Lake of Two Rivers, Hwy. 60, Km. 33.2, 705/633-5551 or 866/473-5551, www.killarneylodge.com, mid-May-mid-Oct., $189-379 pp) is the easiest park lodge to reach, just off Highway 60. With no TVs, radios, or phones, the 25 log cottages are set in the woods, with neat knotty-pine or rough-hewn log interiors. The "one-bedroom" cabins are one room with a king or queen bed; the "two-bedroom" cabins have two rooms, one with a king bed, a second with twin beds. Many cottages are right on the lake, and each comes with its own canoe. Rates include three meals a day.

Ranger Cabins

Algonquin has 14 **Ranger Cabins** (mid-Apr.-mid-Oct., $63-138) that offer indoor camping. They're rustic log structures without running water or electricity where rangers patrolling the park would overnight. You can reach five by car, at Rain Lake, Bissett Creek Road, Kiosk, and two cabins at Brent; others are in the backcountry. Equipped with a table and chairs, a wood stove, and an outdoor toilet,

a cottage at Algonquin's Killarney Lodge

most cabins have bunks but not mattresses, so bring a sleeping pad and a sleeping bag, along with any cooking supplies you want. The Friends of Algonquin Park website (www.algonquinpark.on.ca) has detailed descriptions of each cabin.

Camping

Algonquin is a popular destination for campers, with the largest number of campsites—more than 1,300—of any Ontario provincial park. **Reserve your campsite** (519/826-5290 or 888/668-7275, www.ontarioparks.com/reservations, tent sites $40-44, electrical sites $50, reservation fee online $11, by phone $13) in advance, particularly for summer and fall weekends. Eight of the front-country campgrounds are accessible by car near Highway 60. Most are seasonal, opening in late April or mid-May and closing between early September and mid-October. Only the Mew Lake campground is open year-round.

The front-country campgrounds:

- **Tea Lake** (Km. 11.4, 42 sites) has showers and flush toilets.

- **Canisbay Lake** (Km. 23.1, 242 sites) has secluded campsites, swimming beaches, showers, flush toilets, and laundry facilities.

- **Mew Lake** (Km. 30.6, 131 sites), which has central flush toilets, showers, and laundry, also has seven yurts ($98), available year-round. The yurts, which sleep six, are furnished with two sets of bunk beds (a double below and a single above), a table and chairs, a propane barbecue, cooking utensils, and dishes. They have electric lights and heating. You still need to bring sleeping bags or other bedding, as well as food and other personal items.

- **Two Rivers** (Km. 31.8, 241 sites) is the most centrally located, and frequently the most crowded. It has a beach, a laundry, flush toilets, and showers.

- **Pog Lake** (Km. 36.9, 286 sites) has secluded campsites and central showers, laundry, and flush toilets.

- **Kearney Lake** (Km. 36.5, 103 sites) has two beaches, showers, and flush toilets.

- **Coon Lake** (6 kilometers south of Km. 40.3, 48 sites) has a beach and pit toilets.

- **Rock Lake** (8 kilometers south of Km. 40.3, 121 sites) has two beaches, showers, flush toilets, and laundry.

Algonquin has three more drive-in campgrounds (late Apr.-mid-Oct.) farther north. **Achray** (45 sites), **Brent** (30 sites), and **Kiosk** (22 sites) campgrounds are all accessible from Highway 17 but far more secluded than the Highway 60 camping areas. Achray and Kiosk have flush toilets, and Achray also has a yurt, but none of these three campgrounds has showers.

Algonquin Park also has numerous **backcountry campgrounds** (adults $12, ages 6-17 $5); most are accessible only by canoe. The Friends of Algonquin Park (www.algonquinpark.on.ca) has detailed information to help plan a trip into the backcountry. Several outfitters also organize backcountry trips.

East of the Park

A short drive outside the park's East Gate, the **Couples Resort** (139 Galeairy Lake Rd., Whitney, 866/202-1179, www.couplesresort.ca, $246-838 d), on the waterfront, is unabashedly romantic. Some of the large rooms have four-poster beds, hot tubs or whirlpool baths, and wood-burning fireplaces. Enjoy the seasonal outdoor heated saltwater pool, play billiards or table tennis, take a sauna, or use the fitness room and spa. Midweek specials can reduce the rates significantly. Rates include breakfast and a semiformal five-course dinner; for the evening meal, jeans, shorts, and sandals are forbidden, and men must wear a dress shirt with a collar.

Food

If you're not a lodge guest, you can still come for a meal in the dining room at **Arowhon Pines** (Arowhon Rd., 705/633-5661 or 866/633-5661, www.arowhonpines.ca, late May-mid-Oct.), where meals are fixed-price:

breakfast (8am-10am, $25 pp), weekday lunch (12:30pm-2pm, $35 pp), weekend lunch buffet (12:30pm-2pm, $50 pp), and an abundant multicourse dinner (6:30pm only, $75 pp). The dining room doesn't have a license to serve alcohol, but you can bring your own.

The **Bartlett Lodge Dining Room** (Cache Lake, 705/633-5543 or 866/614-5355, www.bartlettlodge.com, mid-May-late Oct.) is open to nonguests for breakfast ($17.50 pp) and in the evening, when an elaborate five-course prix-fixe dinner ($65 pp) is served; kids have a three-course dinner option ($25 pp). The dining room isn't licensed to serve alcohol, but you can bring your own.

The main lodge building at **Killarney Lodge** (Lake of Two Rivers, Hwy. 60, Km. 33.2, 705/633-5551 or 866/473-5551, www.killarneylodge.com, mid-May-mid-Oct.) dates to 1935 and now houses the dining room, open to nonguests and serving hearty, fixed-price, three-course menus at lunch (noon-2pm daily, $25) and dinner (5:45pm-7:30pm daily, $60). If you're not a lodge guest, reservations are advised for dinner. Also, the dining room keeps slightly shorter hours in May-June, so phone to confirm.

You can get casual meals at the **Portage Store** (Canoe Lake, Hwy. 60, Km. 14.1, 705/633-5622, www.portagestore.com), which serves breakfast, lunch, and dinner daily late April-mid-October, and at the **Sunday Creek Café** (Hwy. 60, Km. 63, 613/637-1133), the basic cafeteria in the Algonquin Visitors Centre. A seasonal snack bar sells sandwiches and ice cream at the **Two Rivers Store** (Hwy. 60, Km. 31.4).

INFORMATION AND SERVICES

For questions about Algonquin Park, phone the **Algonquin Park Information Office** (705/633-5572, 8am-4pm daily). You can also get visitor information at the park's West Gate, East Gate, and Visitors Centre. Online, the best source of information is the **Friends of Algonquin Park** (www.algonquinpark.on.ca). **Ontario Parks** (www.

ontarioparks.com) will give you an overview of the park facilities but doesn't provide as much detail.

Mobile phones do work in Algonquin Park, if you're within about three kilometers (two miles) of Highway 60. There are dead spots, though, and outside this zone, don't count on picking up a phone signal. Within the park, three stores sell camping supplies (including mosquito repellent, rain ponchos, and basic first aid) and a small selection of groceries. The **Portage Store** (Km. 14.1) is on the west end of Highway 60 at Canoe Lake, the **Two Rivers Store** (Km. 31.4) at the Lake of Two Rivers Campground is at roughly the midway point on Highway 60, and the **Opeongo Store** is to the east, a short drive north of Km. 46.3.

GETTING THERE
Car

Algonquin's West Gate is 45 kilometers (28 miles) east of Huntsville via Highway 60. The East Gate is five kilometers (three miles) west of the town of Whitney. From Toronto (270 kilometers, or 168 miles), the most direct, if most heavily trafficked, route is to take Highway 400 north to Highway 11 north, which will take you to Huntsville, where you can take Highway 60 to the West Gate.

An alternate route from Toronto takes you to the East Gate. Go east on Highway 401, then pick up Highway 115 to Peterborough; from there, take Highway 28 north to Bancroft, Highway 62 north to Maynooth, then Highway 127 north to Highway 60, which will bring you to the park's East Gate. While this route sounds more complicated, it's clearly marked; it's about 310 kilometers (190 miles) from Toronto. From Ottawa, it's 240 kilometers (150 miles) to the East Gate; take Highway 417/17 west to Highway 60.

You can buy gas at the Portage Store (Km. 14.1, early May-mid-Oct.). Otherwise, the nearest gas stations are in Oxtongue Lake and Dwight west of the park, and in Whitney to the east.

Bus

The **Parkbus** (800/928-7101, www.parkbus.ca) provides direct bus service from Toronto to Algonquin (one-way adults $60, seniors and students $54, ages 2-12 $30, round-trip adults $85, seniors and students $77, ages 2-12 $43). It's an excellent nonprofit initiative designed to get people out of the city—and out of their cars—by offering transportation to a growing number of national parks and Ontario provincial parks. The bus runs on selected weekends throughout the summer season. The bus departs from several points in Toronto, including 30 Carlton Street (between Yonge St. and Church St., 1 block from the College subway station) and Dufferin Street at Bloor Street West, which is at Dufferin subway station. The Parkbus can also take you from Ottawa to Algonquin. You can catch the bus in downtown Ottawa from the Rideau Centre (50 Rideau St.) or west of downtown at the Mountain Equipment Co-op store (366 Richmond Rd.).

You can get off the bus at several points, including the Wolf Den Hostel near Oxtongue Lake, the West Gate, the Portage Store at Canoe Lake, Lake of Two Rivers Campground, Pog Lake, and the Algonquin Outfitters store on Lake Opeongo. These locations either have accommodations (you can camp at Lake of Two Rivers or Pog Lake, or bunk at the Wolf Den), or they're departure points for outfitters who organize guided trips. The Parkbus works with several outfitters, so you can buy an all-inclusive trip if you prefer.

GETTING AROUND

There is no public transportation within Algonquin Park. If you arrive on the **Parkbus** (800/928-7101, www.parkbus.ca), you can camp at Lake of Two Rivers or Pog Lake, which are both centrally located and have hiking, cycling, and canoeing options nearby, so it's feasible to do without a car. You can also arrive by bus and do a canoeing or hiking trip that you've booked through an outfitter; the bus will drop you at one of several outfitters' locations.

Otherwise, unless you're comfortable bicycling or hiking long distances, you need a car to explore the park. The most convenient place to rent a car in the vicinity of the park is in Huntsville.

North Bay to James Bay

Traveling north from Algonquin Provincial Park or northeast from the Ottawa Valley, the towns get farther apart and the forests get denser. Mining and logging have historically formed the backbone of local economies here, but tourism, particularly outdoor adventure and ecotourism, is a growing business. From the city of North Bay, it's a short trip to the lake town of Temagami, which has excellent canoe-trip options. Farther north, you can board the train for a unique journey to First Nations communities along James Bay.

For more regional travel details, contact **Northeastern Ontario Tourism** (2009 Long Lake Rd., Unit 401, Sudbury, 705/522-0104 or 800/465-6655, www.northeasternontario.com).

NORTH BAY
Sights

On May 28, 1934, quintuplets were born to Oliva and Elzire Dionne, a French Canadian couple living in Corbeil, outside North Bay. These five identical girls—the now-famous Dionne Quintuplets—became an immediate media sensation. By an act of Parliament, they were removed from their parents, who already had five other children under age seven, and designated wards of the Ontario government, which built an "observation playground" where the quints lived—in view of more than three million visitors—until 1943. Although they were eventually returned to their family, the transition to normal life was difficult, and their treatment eventually drew public indignation. The house where the quints were born, which was moved to its current location adjacent to North Bay's Regional Tourist Information Centre east of downtown, is now the **Dionne Quints Museum** (1375 Seymour St., 705/472-8480 or 888/249-8998, www.northbaychamber.com, 9am-7pm daily July-Aug., 9am-5pm Mon.-Fri. and 10am-4pm Sat.-Sun. mid-May-June and Sept.-mid-Oct., adults $3.75, seniors and ages 13-18 $3.25, ages 5-12 $2.25, families $11), filled with memorabilia about their lives and information about their complicated history.

The **Heritage Railway and Carousel** (Memorial Dr., 4pm-dusk Fri., 10am-dusk Sat.-Sun. mid-May-late June, 10am-dusk daily late June-early Sept., 10am-dusk Sat.-Sun. early Sept.-mid-Oct., $2) is an old-time miniature train and merry-go-round that will appeal to kids. In the former train station, the **Discovery North Bay Museum** (100 Ferguson St., 705/476-2323, www.discoverynorthbay.com, 10am-6pm Tues.-Fri., 8am-3pm Sat., adults $7, seniors and students $6, ages 5-12 $5) has model trains and other changing exhibits. Lake Nipissing is a short walk from downtown, and you can explore the lake on a sightseeing cruise aboard the *Chief Commanda II* (200 Memorial Dr., 705/494-8167 or 866/660-6686, www.georgianbaycruise.com, mid-May-early Oct., adults $32, seniors and students $29, youth 13-16 $22, kids 5-12 $16).

Accommodations and Food

Chain motels line Lakeshore Drive south of the city center, including **Super 8 North Bay** (570 Lakeshore Dr., 705/495-4551, www.super8.com, $100-135 d). Off Highway 11, there's **Hampton Inn North Bay** (950 McKeown Ave., 705/474-8400 , www.hamptoninn.hilton.com, $118-159 d) and **Holiday Inn Express & Suites North Bay** (1325 Seymour St., 705/476-7700, www.ihg.com/holidayinnexpress, $121-159 d).

Main Street has several eateries, including the vegetarian-friendly **Cedar Tree Lebanese Restaurant** (183 Main St. E., 705/472-2405, www.cedartreelebaneserestaurant.com, 11am-8pm Mon.-Sat., $5-18), which serves tasty falafel, tabbouleh, *shawarma*, and other Middle Eastern classics.

Information and Services

North Bay's **Regional Tourist Information Centre** (1375 Seymour St., at Hwy. 11,

North Bay's Heritage Carousel

Nipping into Nipissing

The big woods of Algonquin give way to farm country as you drive north on Highway 11, then turn west toward the small village of Nipissing (pronounced "NIH-pih-sing"). Nipissing is attracting modern-day pioneers who are simultaneously getting back to the land and welcoming visitors into their lives. It's a funky, little-touristed destination for a weekend getaway.

Pop in for a quick look through the quirky **Nipissing Museum** (Hwy. 654 at Hwy. 534, 705/724-2938, 10am-4pm Tues.-Sun. mid-June-early Sept., donation), and you may find you're there for an hour or more. The museum was a labor of love for the local resident nicknamed "Museum Joe," who assembled several buildings packed with artifacts reflecting life in Nipissing since the early 1900s. There's the dress of a local woman who met with British royalty, the cash register from the general store, a wide variety of household items, and scads of photos.

The family-run **Board's Honey Farm** (6866 Hwy. 534, 705/729-2939 or 888/363-2827, www. boardshoneyfarm.com, 10am-5pm May-Oct.), between Nipissing and Restoule, houses more than 300 colonies of bees and sells a variety of homemade honeys and honey products. On Thursday in July and August, you can take a guided tour of the beekeeping operations (1:30pm); otherwise, explore the gardens, walking trails, and hives on your own.

Continue west of Highway 534 to quiet **Restoule Provincial Park** (705/729-2010, www. ontarioparks.com), where you can swim in the lake and perhaps spot deer, moose, or other wildlife nearby.

WHERE TO STAY AND EAT

Staying at the **Piebird Bed & Breakfast** (113 Chapman's Landing Rd., 705/724-1144, www. piebird.ca, $125-150 d) is like escaping to a laid-back farm run by your cool, socially conscious friends. Upstairs in the 100-year-old farmhouse are three country bedrooms, two with queen beds and one with a single. They share a bath with an old claw-foot tub; there's also a solar shower outside. A separate cottage on the property ($165) has a full kitchen and bath.

Piebird owners Sherry and Yan, who grow their own vegetables, share their love of organic farming with guests. They serve vegetarian breakfasts, and they'll prepare lunches and dinners by reservation. Even if you're not staying here, you can book a meal if your group includes at least four (or if you're able to join an existing group). They also organize workshops about vegetarian food, herbs, canning, and other topics related to organic and local food, and they host periodic concerts, including the annual **Picnic and Garden Concert,** a day of music and outdoor eating; check their website for details.

GETTING THERE

Nipissing is 340 kilometers (210 miles) north of Toronto and 110 kilometers (68 miles) beyond Huntsville. Turn off Highway 11 at Highway 534 and continue west for about 13 kilometers (eight miles). For Nipissing Village, go north on Highway 654; Highway 534 continues west toward Restoule.

705/472-8480 or 888/249-8998, www.cityof-northbay.ca, 9am-7pm daily July-Aug., 9am-5pm Mon.-Fri. and 10am-4pm Sat.-Sun. mid-May-June and Sept.-mid-Oct., 9am-5pm Mon.-Fri. and 10am-2pm Sat.-Sun. mid-Oct.-mid-May) can assist with information about the area.

Getting There and Around

At the junction of Highways 11 and 17, North Bay is roughly equidistant to Toronto and Ottawa (355 kilometers, or 220 miles), and 130 kilometers (80 miles) east of Sudbury. **Ontario Northland** (www.ontarionorth-land.ca) has bus service to Toronto, while **Greyhound** (www.greyhound.ca) runs buses to Sudbury and Ottawa. The **bus station** (100 Station Rd., 705/495-4200) is east of downtown, near Highway 17.

You really need a car to explore North Bay.

Local rental agencies include **Avis** (705/476-9730, www.avis.com), **Enterprise** (705/840-7777, www.enterprise.com), and **National** (705/474-3030, www.nationalcar.com).

SUDBURY

Sudbury reveals its charms slowly. This industrial city of 160,000 is ringed with the belching smokestacks and rocky pits of its many active mines. Yet if you find yourself here, en route to Sault Ste. Marie, Manitoulin Island, Killarney Provincial Park, or wilderness spots farther north, it's worth exploring. The city's science museum is a don't-miss sight if you have children in tow, and the compact downtown has a handful of interesting restaurants and galleries, including **Artists on Elgin** (168 Elgin St., 705/674-0415, www.artistsonelgin. ca, 10am-5pm Mon.-Sat.), which features local artists' work.

★ Science North

Kids (and their parents) could easily spend a day or more at Sudbury's cool, contemporary science museum, **Science North** (100 Ramsey Lake Rd., 705/523-4629 or 800/461-4898, www.sciencenorth.ca, 9am-6pm daily late June-early Sept., 10am-4pm daily early Sept.-Dec., call or check the website for hours winter-spring; adults $25, seniors and ages 13-17 $23, ages 3-12 $21).

Built into a massive rock on the edge of Ramsey Lake (you enter the exhibit halls through a tunnel blasted from the bedrock), this year-round hands-on museum is packed with "please touch" exhibits, focusing on the environment, animals, the human body, and more. In the Nature Exchange, kids can bring in something they've found—a plant, a rock, a bug—learn something about it, and exchange it for something in the museum's collection. Many exhibitions highlight the wildlife, plants, geology, and ecology of Northern Ontario.

Admission packages including Science North and the on-site IMAX theatre or planetarium are available, as are combination tickets to Science North and Dynamic Earth.

Dynamic Earth

In a region where mining, primarily for nickel and copper, is such a big part of the local economy, it's no surprise that a major attraction is the high-tech mining museum **Dynamic Earth** (122 Big Nickel Rd., 705/523-4629 or 800/461-4898, www.dynamicearth.ca, Mar.-Oct., call or check the website for winter hours, adults $20, seniors and ages 13-17 $18, ages 3-12 $16).

A highlight is the 45-minute Underground Tour through a simulated mine, where you walk through 100 years of mining technology, from the dark, narrow tunnels of the early 1900s to the more high-tech mines of today. It's a rather promotional pitch for the mining industry but still makes for an interesting tour. Another fun exhibit is the Mining Command Centre, where you use computers to drill or smash rocks and track mine activities (you can even spy on the Underground Tour groups). Outside, the **Big Nickel,** a really big 13-ton replica of a 1951 Canadian five-cent piece, symbolizes the importance of nickel production to Sudbury's, and Canada's, economy.

Dynamic Earth operates in conjunction with Science North, and you can buy a combination ticket to both; the two attractions are about five kilometers (three miles) apart.

Entertainment and Events

Sudbury hosts a variety of arts festivals, including **Northern Lights Festival Boreal** (www.nlfbsudbury.com, July), a long-running music fest on Ramsey Lake; the **Cinéfest Sudbury International Film Festival** (www.cinefest.com, Sept.), and the **Sudbury Jazz Festival** (www.jazzsudbury. ca, Sept.). A unique food-and-music party is the **Canadian Garlic Festival** (www.ukrseniors.org, Aug.), sponsored by the Ukrainian Seniors Centre; bring your own breath mints.

Accommodations

The "artisan" at the **Artisan Upstairs Guesthouse** (318 Jeanne D'Arc Ave., 705/674-4387, www.artisanupstairs.com,

$100 s, $130 d), on a residential street east of downtown, is co-owner Pete Lautenschlager, who carved much of the furniture and woodwork in these two second-floor guest rooms. Popular with couples and business travelers, the bedrooms have sponge-painted walls and private baths. Guests can use the fully equipped kitchenette and relax on the deck overlooking the nearby woods. Rates include full breakfast.

The **Southbay Guesthouse Sudbury** (1802 Southbay Rd., 705/859-2363, www.southbayguesthouse.com) has an enviable waterfront location in a private home on Ramsey Lake. The larger Luna de Miel suite ($155 d) has a king bed, two-person whirlpool tub, and a fireplace, while the queen-bed Sunrise suite ($139 d) opens onto a lakeside deck. Rates include breakfast. The same family runs Manitoulin Island's Southbay Guesthouse.

Among the nicest of Sudbury's many chain motels along Regent Street south of downtown is the 121-room **Hampton Inn-Sudbury** (2280 Regent St., 705/523-5200, www.sudburyontario.hamptoninn.com, $127-159 d), which makes both business travelers and vacationing families feel at home. The beds are topped with crisp white duvets, and kids will appreciate the indoor pool.

Food

Head downtown around Durham Street for a selection of restaurants and cafés. A seasonal **farmers market** (233 Elgin St., 705/674-4455, www.greatersudbury.ca/market, 8am-2pm Sat., 10am-2pm Sun., late June-Oct.) operates outside the downtown rail station.

The name is fitting at **Café Petit Gateau** (149 Durham St., 705/222-2233, www.cafepetitgateau.com, 9am-5pm Tues.-Fri., 10am-4pm Sat.), a tiny shop that bakes a changing assortment of cookies, scones, cakes, and other sweets to pair with tea or espresso drinks. **Fromagerie Elgin** (5 Cedar St., at Elgin, 705/675-1000, www.fromagerieelgin.ca, 10am-9pm Mon.-Sat., 11am-3pm Sun., $6-12) is part cheese shop and part café, where patrons settle into the long wooden table for cheese plates, sandwiches, and daily-changing soups. They host art exhibits and regular live music nights, too; call for schedules. At **Leinala's** (272 Caswell Dr., 705/522-1977), a traditional Finnish bakery, it's difficult to choose among the delicious sweet breads and fresh-cooked doughnuts, including their specialty, jelly pigs (glazed and filled with jam). It's in a strip mall off Regent Street, south of downtown.

A chill downtown spot for vegetarians and their nonveg companions is the **Laughing Buddha** (194 Elgin St., 705/673-2112, www.laughingbuddhasudbury.com, 11am-2am daily), a café-bar that hums till the wee hours. Whether you want herbal tea or booze, a Treehugger Salad (a hearty bowl of romaine, tomatoes, mushrooms, raisins, and cashews) or a Swiss and Sow (a ham and cheese sandwich), the laid-back staff will oblige.

Information and Services
Sudbury Tourism (200 Brady St., 705/674-4455, ext. 7718, or 866/451-8252, www.sudburytourism.ca) has details about the city on its website.

Getting There
Sudbury is well served with air, train, and bus connections, but all its transportation terminals are inconveniently located outside the city center.

AIR
The **Greater Sudbury Airport** (YSB, 5000 Air Terminal Dr., Garson, 705/693-2514 or 855/359-2972, www.flysudbury.ca) is 25 kilometers (15 miles) northeast of downtown. **Air Canada** (www.aircanada.com) flies to Toronto's Pearson Airport, but you can sometimes find better deals on **Porter Airlines** (www.flyporter.com) to Toronto's City Airport. **Bearskin Airlines** (705/693-9199 or 800/465-2327, www.bearskinairlines.com) serves Ottawa, Sault Ste. Marie, and Thunder Bay.

From the airport to in-town hotels, **Sudbury Cab** (705/626-7968, www.

sudburycab.com) runs both shared-van shuttles ($40-60) and taxis ($50-73). You must book shuttles at least one day in advance.

TRAIN
VIA Rail's transcontinental Toronto-Vancouver train stops two or three days a week at **Sudbury Junction** (2750 Lasalle Blvd., 705/524-1591), 10 kilometers (six miles) northeast of the city center. The Sudbury-Toronto leg (one-way adults $64-103) takes 7-8 hours. Note that the only trains using the **Sudbury Downtown Station** (233 Elgin St.) travel to the town of White River, between Sault Ste. Marie and Thunder Bay.

BUS
From Sudbury's **Intercity Bus Terminal** (854 Notre Dame Ave., 705/524-9900), three kilometers (1.9 miles) north of downtown, **Ontario Northland** (www.ontarionorthland.ca) runs buses to Toronto (5.5-6 hours, one-way adults $73.15, seniors and students $62.20, children $36.60) and north to Cochrane (6 hours, one-way adults $74.25, seniors and students $63.10, children $37.10). **Greyhound** (www.greyhound.ca) connects Sudbury with Sault Ste. Marie (4.5 hours, one-way adults $54-86) and Toronto (5-5.5 hours, one-way adults $46-97). A taxi from the bus station to downtown will cost about $15.

CAR
Sudbury is at the intersection of Highway 69 to Toronto and Highway 17, which goes west to Sault Ste. Marie and east to North Bay and Ottawa. The city is 390 kilometers (242 miles) north of Toronto, a five- to six-hour drive. Sudbury is 90 minutes north of Killarney Provincial Park and about the same distance to Manitoulin Island's swing bridge.

Getting Around
Although the city center is compact and walkable, Sudbury's attractions are all outside downtown. You can get around by bus (if you're patient) or taxi, but having your own wheels is more convenient. **Greater**

Sudbury Transit (705/675-3333, www.greatersudbury.ca) runs the city's bus network. Local cab companies include **Lockerby Taxi** (705/522-2222, www.lockerbytransportation.com) and **Aaron Taxi** (705/523-3333, www.aaronservices.ca/taxi). **Avis** (www.avis.ca), **Enterprise** (www.enterpriserentacar.ca), and **Budget** (www.budget.ca) are among Sudbury's car rental options.

★ TEMAGAMI
If you love to canoe or hike, Temagami, a wilderness region dotted with lakes large and small, makes a great getaway. Outdoor adventurers flock here in summer, increasing the population from 1,000 to over 10,000. Paddlers will find scores of opportunities for multiday canoe trips. If it's winter in the outdoors you crave, Temagami can oblige, with snowshoeing, cross-country skiing, and dogsledding. Local outfitters help organize active trips.

The town's name, pronounced "Teh-MAW-gah-mee," is an Ojibwa word, roughly translated as "Deep Water by the Shore," a fitting moniker for this lake country.

Sights
For an expansive aerial view of the surrounding lakes and forests, climb the 30-meter (100-foot) **Temagami Fire Tower** ($3). At 396 meters (1,300 feet) above sea level, it's the highest point on Yonge Street (Hwy. 11), which runs more or less all the way to Toronto (and at one time was named the longest street in the world).

Two kilometers (1.2 miles) south of town, **Finlayson Point Park** (24 Finlayson Park Rd., off Hwy. 11, 705/569-3205, www.ontarioparks.com, late May-late Sept., $14.50 per vehicle) has two small sandy swimming beaches on Lake Temagami. You can also rent canoes or explore the park's hiking trails. A museum has exhibits about the park's natural environment.

A vast protected wilderness surrounds Temagami, with a network of backcountry parks. The largest is **Lady Evelyn**

Smoothwater Provincial Park (www.ontarioparks.com) to the northwest. Exploring this rugged region isn't for outdoor novices; you need backcountry camping, white-water canoeing, and other wilderness skills. Contact local outfitters for information about backcountry trips.

Sports and Recreation

Smoothwater Wilderness Lodge (705/569-3539 or 888/569-4539, www.smoothwater.com) can organize canoe, kayak, or hiking adventures. The **Temagami Outfitting Company** (6 Lakeshore Dr., 705/569-2595, www.icanoe.ca) runs an outdoor gear store and plans canoe, kayak, and hiking trips. **Lakeland Airways** (705/569-3455, www.lakelandairways.ca) can take you into the wilderness surrounding Temagami by floatplane. They'll even strap your canoe to the plane and drop you off on a remote lake.

Another way to explore is by houseboat, which you can pilot along the interconnected lakes that wind through the region. Contact **Leisure Island Houseboat Rentals** (705/569-3261, www.leisureislandhouseboats.com) or **Three Buoys Houseboat Rentals** (705/569-3455, www.threebuoyshouseboats.ca) for rentals.

For winter excursions, contact **Wolf Within Adventures** (705/840-9002, www.wolfwithin.ca), which runs dogsledding expeditions with a team of Alaskan huskies.

Accommodations and Food

Temagami's best place to stay is the ★ **Smoothwater Wilderness Lodge** (Smoothwater Rd., off Hwy. 11, 705/569-3539 or 888/569-4539, www.smoothwater.com, $30 dorm, $140 d, packages available). The rustic petite doubles and bunkhouse are comfortable, staff are friendly and knowledgeable, and family-style breakfasts ($15) and dinners ($55) feature local ingredients. Adventures include paddling on the property's lake and multiday canoeing and camping excursions. In winter, you can snowshoe or cross-country ski on 50 kilometers (31 miles) of trails. Lounge

Climb the Temagami Fire Tower for views of the surrounding lakes.

lakeside or in the Gathering Hall with comfy sofas, books, and games. Smoothwater is 14 kilometers (8.7 miles) north of Temagami.

Shops and restaurants are clustered along Highway 11 and on Lakeshore Drive, bordering Lake Temagami. Although the sign at this roadside stand says **B&D Burgers** (6731 Hwy. 11, $2.50-12), everyone calls it "The Chip Shop," because that's what you should order: chips (french fries), specifically the French Canadian specialty known as *poutine*. You can get a hamburger, hot dog, or fried fish, if you must, but it's the mounds of fries topped with gooey cheese and brown gravy that keep the picnic tables packed. When they ask if you want "shredded or curds" on your *poutine,* they're inquiring about the cheese; to be authentic, you want curds.

CAMPING

Finlayson Point Park (Finlayson Park Rd., off Hwy. 11, 705/569-3205, www.ontarioparks.com, late May-late Sept., tent sites $35-40, electrical sites $40-46) has 117 campsites, many right on Lake Temagami. The campground has showers, flush toilets, and laundry facilities. The park also rents a two-bedroom **cabin** ($170) with log furniture and an electric fireplace; it has no plumbing, but it's a short walk to the washrooms.

Campers are welcome to pitch a tent on the lawn at **Smoothwater Wilderness Lodge** (705/569-3539 or 888/569-4539, www.smooth-water.com, $15); you can use the restrooms and showers in the bunkhouse.

Practicalities

The **Temagami Chamber of Commerce Information Centre** (7 Lakeshore Dr., 705/569-3344 or 800/661-7609, www.temagamiinformation.com) can give you information about the area. Temagami is 455 kilometers (285 miles) north of Toronto and 100 kilometers (60 miles) north of North Bay. **Ontario Northland** (www.ontarionorthland.ca) operates two buses a day between Toronto and **Temagami station** (Hwy. 11, 705/569-3310, 8 hours, one-way adults $104.40, seniors and students $88.75, children $52.25) and from Temagami on to Cochrane (5-5.25 hours, one-way adults $73.35, seniors and students $62.40, children $36.70).

COCHRANE

The main reason to come to Cochrane is to leave again. This windswept town with a remote, almost Wild West feel, is the starting point for the *Polar Bear Express* train that runs north toward James Bay, at the edge of the Arctic.

While Cochrane isn't far enough north to support arctic wildlife, the town capitalizes on its polar bear connection as the home of the small **Polar Bear Habitat and Heritage Village** (1 Drury Park Rd., 705/272-2327 or 800/354-9948, www.polarbearhabitat.ca, 9am-5pm daily May-Oct., 10am-4pm daily Nov.-Apr., adults $16, seniors $14, students $12, ages 5-11 $10, families $45), a polar bear sanctuary and research facility. A highlight for visitors is swimming with the bears—on the other side of a clear enclosure. Because the

bear population at the sanctuary fluctuates, check the status before making a special trip; in 2014 there were two bears in residence. Also on the grounds is a modest one-street heritage village and a snowmobile museum.

If you still have time to kill, visit the **Tim Horton Museum** (7 Tim Horton Dr., off 4th St. E., 705/272-5084, call for hours, $2), inside the Tim Horton Event Centre, 2.5 kilometers (1.6 miles) east of the station. Born in Cochrane in 1930, Horton played 22 seasons in the National Hockey League, but he's equally well known as the founder of the ubiquitous Canadian doughnut shop chain that bears his name.

For visitor information, look for the giant polar bear. Chimo, an 11-meter (35-foot) bear statue (its name is an Inuit word meaning "welcome"), greets visitors outside the **Town of Cochrane Information Centre** (3 3rd Ave./Hwy. 11, 705/272-4926, www.town.cochrane.on.ca).

Accommodations and Food

Cochrane's accommodations are clustered near the train station, with additional chain motels on Highway 11 south of town. Behind a grim stone facade is Cochrane's most upscale lodging, the **Best Western Swan Castle Inn** (189 Railway St., 705/272-5200 or 800/265-3668, www.bestwesternontario.com, $130-150 d), which has 39 middle-of-the-road rooms and a helpful staff. Rates include continental breakfast.

You can roll out of bed and onto your train from the **Station Inn** (200 Railway St., 705/272-3500 or 800/265-2356, www.ontarionorthland.ca, $105-115 d), with 23 smallish rooms above the depot. The **coffee shop** ($5-16) serves three meals daily, from eggs and sandwiches to pastas and pork chops. The low-rise **Commando Motel** (80 7th Ave. S., 705/272-2700, www.commandomotel.com, $65 s, $70 d) is another option, with free Wi-Fi, one block from the station.

To rustle up some grub, your best bet is the **J.R. Bar-B-Q Ranch** (63 3rd Ave., 705/272-4999, 11am-9pm Mon.-Sat., 3pm-8pm Sun.),

Where's the Factory on Moose Factory?

The James Bay region in Northern Ontario has been traditional Cree territory for thousands of years. More recently (in the 17th century, that is), the Hudson's Bay Company established Ontario's first English-speaking settlement on Moose Factory Island, just south of James Bay. Traders came to the island in 1673, which makes Moose Factory Ontario's oldest fur-trading community.

It was this fur-trading heritage that gave the island its unusual name. The "Moose" referred to the Moose River, where the island is located, but there wasn't (and still isn't) a factory on the island, at least in the modern sense of the word. In the 17th century, the chief agent at a fur-trading post was called a "factor." And the place where a factor worked was called a "factory."

Today, little of this fur-trading era remains on Moose Factory Island. On Front Street, near the Quickstop Convenience Store, is the **Hudson's Bay Staff House** that was once part of the Hudson's Bay Post. A more permanent legacy, perhaps, is the island **cemetery** (Pehdabun Rd.) where some of these early settlers were laid to rest.

---

where the family-friendly room, decorated with saddles and trophy fish, feels like the love child of a cowboy and a north-woods fisherman. The hearty barbecued ribs (half rack $18, full rack $24) are worth hooting over, and the menu includes ample portions of barbecue chicken, burgers, steaks, and pizza.

Getting There and Around

Cochrane is off Highway 11, 725 kilometers (450 miles) north of Toronto and 375 kilometers (235 miles) beyond North Bay. *Polar Bear Express* passengers who've arrived in Cochrane by car can leave their vehicles in the station parking lot during their journey north.

Cochrane Station (200 Railway St., 705/272-4228) is both the train station and the depot for **Ontario Northland** buses from Toronto (www.ontarionorthland.ca, 12-13 hours, one-way adults $160.75, seniors and students $136.65, ages 2-11 $80.35), a long haul via Huntsville, North Bay, and Temagami. Cochrane has no public transit, but you can easily walk around the small town.

★ POLAR BEAR EXPRESS TRAIN

You won't see polar bears en route (it's still too far south), nor is the Ontario Northland train particularly "express," yet this 299-kilometer (186-mile) **rail journey** (800/265-2356, www.ontarionorthland.ca, 5 hours, Sun.-Fri. July-Aug., Mon.-Fri. Sept.-June, one-way adults $59.25, seniors and students $50.40, children $29.65) gives you a fascinating glimpse of life in the north. From Cochrane, the train chugs through stands of birch and poplar toward swampier lowlands dotted with skinny, green-tufted black spruce before pulling into the predominantly Cree community of Moosonee, where you can also visit nearby Moose Factory Island, another Cree settlement.

It's not a luxury train, but there's a dome car with broader views of the surrounding terrain, a dining car, an entertainment car (where local bands often perform), and a family car, offering activities and movies to help kids pass the time. You can rent a worthwhile audio tour ($15) that provides background about the region, points out highlights of Moosonee and Moose Factory Island, and introduces you to Cree culture.

Many people take the *Polar Bear Express* from Cochrane, make a quick tour of Moosonee and Moose Factory Island, and return the same night. If you have time, though, stay at least one or two nights in the north to better experience Cree culture.

In July and August, day-trippers have almost four hours to walk around Moosonee and Moose Factory before the southbound train departs. The rest of the year, the train's tourism amenities are discontinued, and the southbound train leaves three hours after the northbound train arrives, making a day trip less feasible.

Practicalities

The *Polar Bear Express* train departs Cochrane at 9am and reaches **Moosonee Station** (705/336-2210) about five hours later. The return train leaves Moosonee at 6pm in July-August and at 5pm September-June.

Advance reservations are recommended; pay for your tickets at least three days in advance and receive a 10 percent discount. Family discounts may be available for at least one adult and one child traveling together.

Moosonee and Vicinity

If you look at a map of Northeastern Ontario, you'll notice one important thing is missing: roads. The only way to reach the remote area around James Bay, which has a predominantly First Nations population, is by rail or air.

The *Polar Bear Express* train travels to Moosonee, a town of about 3,500 near James Bay. The Moosonee area has two main settlements: the dusty frontier town of Moosonee itself on the mainland, and the island of Moose Factory in the Moose River just offshore. Local websites with information about the region include the **Moose Cree First Nation** (www.moosecree.com) and the town of **Moosonee** (www.moosonee.ca).

Moosonee's main street is 1st Avenue, which runs from the train station to the river, where you can catch a water taxi to Moose Factory Island. Stop first at the **Railway Car Museum** (1st St., July-Aug., free), opposite the station, to check out the exhibits about the area's culture and history. Down the street is **Northern College** (1st St., 705/336-2913, www.northernc.on.ca, 8am-4pm Mon.-Fri., free), where displays of indigenous crafts, including leather and beadwork, line the hallways.

MOOSE FACTORY ISLAND

Home to 2,700 people, Moose Factory is 4.8 kilometers (three miles) long and 3.2 kilometers (two miles) wide; the Moose Cree First Nation Reserve occupies much of the island.

The island's main attraction is the **Cree Cultural Interpretive Centre** (Pehdabun Rd., 705/658-4619, ext. 265, www.moosecree.com, 9am-5pm Sun.-Fri. July-Aug., off-season by appointment, adults $10, under age 12 $5), which has well-designed exhibits about Cree culture, language, traditional medicine, and food. Outside the building, you can peek

native script on the Railway Car Museum, Moosonee

into several tepees. Located on the island's east side, the center is about a 30-minute walk from the Cree Village Ecolodge or from the town docks. The waterfront views along Pehdabun Road are lovely.

In summer, the Cree Village Ecolodge can arrange **boat trips** from Moose Factory to nearby Fossil Island and up to James Bay, 15 kilometers (nine miles) to the north, weather and tides permitting.

The whole island seems to gather at the **Moose Cree Complex** (Mookijuneibeg Dr.), part shopping mall and part community center. There's a grocery store, a pharmacy, a coffee shop, a bank, and a post office, and residents often sell homemade baked goods or crafts. The building also houses the **Moose Cree Tourism Office** (705/658-4619, ext. 265).

ACCOMMODATIONS AND FOOD

Opposite the docks in Moosonee, the friendly **Polar Bear Lodge** (705/336-2345, $115 d) has 27 barebones rooms—half have one double bed, the remainder have two—and a **restaurant** (year-round) that serves three meals a day. In July and August, they run a free shuttle to and from the train station. On 1st Street are the **Northern Store** (a large grocery), a bank,

and the post office. Note the Cree script on signs around town.

It's much nicer to stay on Moose Factory Island, where the Moose Cree First Nation run the ★ **Cree Village Ecolodge** (Hospital Dr., 705/658-6400 or 888/273-3929, www.creevillage.com) on the banks of the Moose River. The 20 rustically comfortable rooms have organic cotton bedding, birch blinds, and Wi-Fi, and the staff help arrange tours. The lodge's showpiece is the dining room—the best place to eat in the area—with a soaring ceiling and a multistory wall of windows facing the water. The kitchen uses traditional First Nations ingredients in its bison chili, baked pickerel, venison, and other dishes ($17-33).

In a teepee opposite the Ecolodge, you'll often find Cree women cooking bannock—a traditional biscuit-like bread—over an open fire. Hours are irregular, so if you see the fire going, stop for a snack. For a casual meal, join the locals at the **Moose Cree Complex Coffee Shop** (Mookijuneibeg Dr., 8am-7pm Mon.-Sat., 9am-7pm Sun., $6-12) for bacon and eggs, sandwiches, and other diner-style chow.

The **Northern Store** (Moose Cree Complex, Mookijuneibeg Dr., 705/658-4552, 10am-6pm Mon.-Wed. and Sat., 10am-8pm

the Moose Cree First Nation run the Cree Village Ecolodge

Thurs.-Fri.) is a well-stocked grocery store, although prices—as in many northern towns—are significantly higher than they are down south. You can also pick up provisions at **G. G.'s Corner** (Center Rd., 705/685-4591, 11am-9pm daily) or **Quickstop Convenience** (Front St., 705/658-4086, noon-7pm daily).

GETTING AROUND

From Moosonee's train station, it's about a 15-20-minute walk to the docks; a taxi will cost about $6. In summer, **water taxis** ($15 pp) cross the river between Moosonee and Moose Factory Island in 10-15 minutes. Boats typically wait at the docks on both the Moosonee and Moose Factory sides. The Cree

Village Ecolodge has its own dock, on the opposite side of the island from the main public dock, so be sure to tell the boatman if you're heading to the lodge.

In midwinter, the river freezes solid enough to support an **ice road** between Moose Factory and the mainland; taxis and other vehicles can drive across. During the fall "freeze-up" and spring "break-up" periods, when the river is too icy for boats to cross but not solid enough for cars, the only way on and off Moose Factory Island is by helicopter.

Taxis typically meet trains arriving in Moosonee. For a cab on Moose Factory Island, call **Creeway** (705/658-5256) or **Northway** (705/658-4131).

Georgian Bay

With Caribbean-blue water, dramatic rock formations, and a network of red-and-white lighthouses standing guard along the shore, some of Ontario's most spectacular scenery surrounds Georgian Bay. If you're looking for a getaway to the outdoors, whether for exhilarating adventure or relaxing by the water, head to this eastern finger of Lake Huron.

Measuring 320 kilometers (200 miles) long and 80 kilometers (50 miles) wide, Georgian Bay is dotted with more than 30,000 islands and some of the finest scuba diving in the north. The region has three national parks, several large provincial parks, ski slopes, and canoe routes, as well as the world's longest freshwater beach. It's a hugely popular destination for hikers, too, encompassing the northern portions of the Bruce Trail, Canada's longest hiking route.

You won't want to miss the stunning Bruce Peninsula, with its unusual rock formations, offshore islands, and network of hiking trails. Georgian Bay Islands National Park is the gateway to the 30,000 Islands region, and splurging on a floatplane tour over the water nearby is a new level of thrill. Winter sports enthusiasts should head to the Blue Mountains, Ontario's top ski and

snowboarding region; the surrounding area draws foodies, too, with numerous top-notch restaurants. If you prefer history and culture with your outdoor adventures, the towns of Midland, Penetanguishene, and Parry Sound will oblige.

Another superlative outdoor destination, Killarney Provincial Park lures paddlers and hikers to its shores studded with pink granite and its trails lined with pines. You can hike the challenging trail to The Crack for views across the hills, or simply spend a morning canoeing on a peaceful inland lake.

On Manitoulin Island, the Great Spirit Circle Trail is a leader in aboriginal tourism, offering experiences in music, dance, traditional medicine, hiking, and more that introduce visitors to First Nations culture and heritage. The world's largest freshwater island, Manitoulin has long sandy beaches,

---

Previous: Killarney Provincial Park; South Baymouth. **Above:** canoeing on Killarney's George Lake.

Look for ★ to find recommended sights, activities, dining, and lodging.

Highlights

★ **Bruce Peninsula National Park:** This national park is among Ontario's most beautiful settings. Its intricate rock formations, turquoise waters, and more than 40 species of orchids draw hikers, kayakers, and other nature lovers (page 56).

★ **The Bruce Trail:** This iconic Canadian hiking route stretches 845 kilometers (525 miles) from the Niagara region to the end of the Bruce Peninsula (page 57).

★ **Fathom Five National Marine Park:** Best known for its distinctive "flowerpot" rock formations and for the shipwrecks where you can snorkel or explore by boat, this national marine conservation area also has some of the finest scuba diving in North America (page 59).

★ **Sainte-Marie Among the Hurons:** This historic village "reimagines" the first European settlement in Ontario, where French Jesuits lived and worked with the indigenous Wendat people in the 1600s (page 80).

★ **Georgian Bay Islands National Park:** Of the thousands of islands that dot Georgian Bay,

63 are protected in this island national park. Visit for a day of hiking and swimming, or stay in a quiet cabin by the shore (page 86).

★ **Flight-Seeing:** The most thrilling way to take in Georgian Bay's 30,000 Islands is on a floatplane tour. Soar above the bay by day or take a romantic sunset flight—complete with champagne (page 90).

★ **Killbear Provincial Park:** This waterfront area near Parry Sound offers granite cliffs, sandy beaches, and a lovely destination for hiking, canoeing, swimming, and camping (page 93).

★ **Killarney Provincial Park:** Escape to the wilderness of this vast and dramatic park, with its rugged white dolomite ridges, pink granite cliffs, pine forests, and crystal-clear lakes (page 95).

★ **Great Spirit Circle Trail:** Explore aboriginal culture on Manitoulin Island, the world's largest freshwater island. Take a guided "Mother Earth" nature hike or a workshop on traditional dance, drumming, or food, and stay on a First Nations reserve (page 100).

Georgian Bay

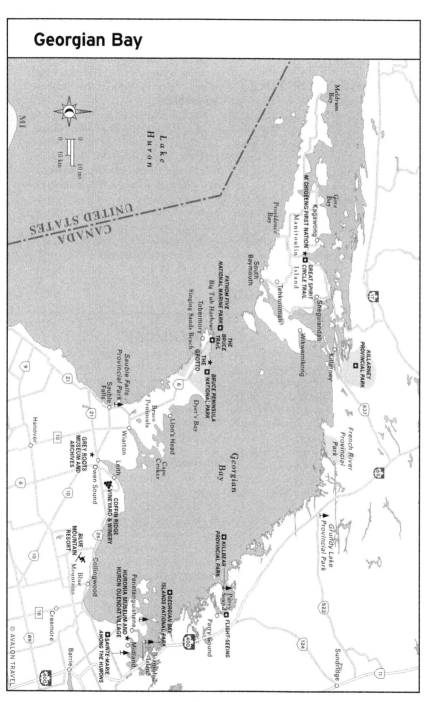

© AVALON TRAVEL

quiet roads for cycling, and—like much of this waterside region—plenty of spots to sit and simply enjoy the bay.

PLANNING YOUR TIME

Many attractions and services around Georgian Bay don't begin operation until mid- or late May and close in mid-October, after the Canadian Thanksgiving weekend. One exception is the Blue Mountains, which draws winter visitors for skiing and snowboarding.

For a long weekend, do a quick tour of the **Bruce Peninsula,** ski or snowboard at **Blue Mountain,** pair a visit to **Midland**'s historic sights with a day trip to **Georgian Bay Islands National Park,** or base yourself in

Parry Sound and explore the nearby provincial parks. You can easily spend 4-5 days on the Bruce Peninsula, particularly if you want to hike sections of the Bruce Trail and snorkel or scuba-dive in the **Fathom Five National Marine Park.**

An excellent way to explore the region is by following the **Georgian Bay Coastal Route,** a complete loop around the bay. From May to October you can take a ferry between the Bruce Peninsula and **Manitoulin Island,** then continue to **Killarney Provincial Park,** the Georgian Bay Islands, Midland, **Wasaga Beach,** and the Blue Mountains. Although you could cover most of this route in a week, you'll have more time for outdoor activities if you can spend at least 10 days.

The Bruce Peninsula

With limestone cliffs, crystal blue waters, forested hiking trails, and even a wide variety of orchids, the Bruce Peninsula's striking natural scenery is the main reason to visit this finger of land that juts out between Lake Huron and Georgian Bay. The must-see attractions are its two national parks—Bruce Peninsula National Park and Fathom Five National Marine Park—at the peninsula's north end, around the town of Tobermory. Yet beyond these natural attractions, it's the friendly, low-key atmosphere that draws vacationers. Though the region attracts plenty of visitors, it hasn't lost its small-town warmth, with people greeting each other on the street and on the trail.

For pre-trip research, check out the detailed **County of Bruce Tourism website** (www.explorethebruce.com), with extensive information about the Bruce Peninsula and surrounding communities. Also pick up the useful **Grey-Bruce Official Visitor Map** (www.explorethebruce.com) at information centers around the region; it shows both major and minor roads across the peninsula.

TOBERMORY

To explore Bruce Peninsula National Park and the Fathom Five National Marine Park, it's most convenient to base yourself in Tobermory, a pretty waterfront town at the northern tip of the Bruce Peninsula. Highway 6, the peninsula's main north-south road, ends in Tobermory.

National Park Visitors Centre

Start your visit at the **National Park Visitors Centre** (120 Chi Sin Tib Dek Rd., 519/596-2233, www.pc.gc.ca, 9am-5pm Sun.-Mon. and Thurs.-Fri., 8am-5pm Sat. mid-May-late June, 8am-8pm daily late June-early Sept., 9am-5pm Thurs.-Mon. early Sept.-mid-Oct., national park admission fee adults $5.80, seniors $4.90, children $2.90, families $14.70), for information about both Bruce Peninsula National Park and Fathom Five National Marine Park. Watch a short film about the area's highlights and explore exhibits about local ecology. Then climb the 112 steps up the 20-meter (65-foot) **Lookout Tower** for views across the peninsula and the nearby islands.

In summer, park staff offer a variety of

The Bruce Peninsula

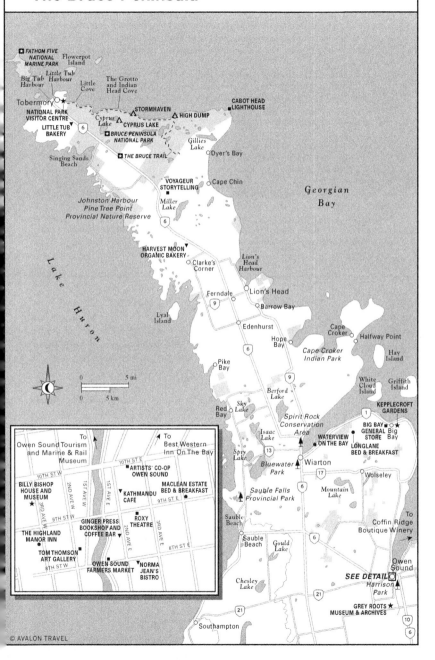

FATHOM FIVE NATIONAL MARINE PARK
Flowerpot Island
Little Tub Harbour
Big Tub Harbour
Little Cove
The Grotto and Indian Head Cove
CABOT HEAD LIGHTHOUSE
Tobermory
NATIONAL PARK VISITOR CENTRE
LITTLE TUB BAKERY
STORMHAVEN
Cyprus Lake
CYPRUS LAKE
HIGH DUMP
BRUCE PENINSULA NATIONAL PARK
Gillies Lake
THE BRUCE TRAIL
Dyer's Bay
Singing Sands Beach
VOYAGEUR STORYTELLING
Cape Chin
Georgian Bay
Johnston Harbour Pine Tree Point Provincial Nature Reserve
Miller Lake
HARVEST MOON ORGANIC BAKERY
Clarke's Corner
Lion's Head Harbour
Lake Huron
Ferndale
Lion's Head
Barrow Bay
Lyal Island
Edenhurst
Cape Croker
Halfway Point
Hope Bay
Cape Croker Indian Park
Hay Island
Pike Bay
White Cloud Island
Griffith Island
Berford Lake
0 5 mi
0 5 km
Red Bay
Sky Lake
Spirit Rock Conservation Area
KEPPLECROFT GARDENS
Isaac Lake
WATERVIEW ON THE BAY
BIG BAY GENERAL STORE
Big Bay
LONGLANE BED & BREAKFAST
Spry Lake
Bluewater Park
Wiarton
Wolseley
Sauble Falls Provincial Park
Mountain Lake
Sauble Beach
To Coffin Ridge Boutique Winery
Sauble Beach
Gould Lake
Owen Sound
SEE DETAIL
Harrison Park
Chesley Lake
GREY ROOTS MUSEUM & ARCHIVES
Southampton

To Owen Sound Tourism and Marine & Rail Museum
To Best Western Inn On The Bay
ARTISTS' CO-OP OWEN SOUND
10TH ST E
10TH ST W
BILLY BISHOP HOUSE AND MUSEUM
KATHMANDU CAFÉ
MACLEAN ESTATE BED & BREAKFAST
9TH ST E
GINGER PRESS BOOKSHOP AND COFFEE BAR
ROXY THEATRE
THE HIGHLAND MANOR INN
TOM THOMSON ART GALLERY
8TH ST W
8TH ST E
OWEN SOUND FARMERS MARKET
NORMA JEAN'S BISTRO

On the Lookout for Lighthouses

What is it about lighthouses that draw people like a beacon? If you're a lighthouse lover, the Lake Huron and Georgian Bay coasts are prime territory for lighthouse touring. Many of the region's lighthouses were built in the mid- to late 1800s or early 1900s during the heyday of Great Lakes shipping.

On Lake Huron, visit the **Chantry Island Light** (www.chantryisland.com) near Southampton and the **Kincardine Lighthouse** (www.sunsets.com), a lighthouse-turned-museum near Kincardine's downtown. The Bruce Peninsula has several lighthouses, including the **Big Tub Lighthouse** in Tobermory, the **Cabot Head Lighthouse and Museum** (www.cabothead.ca), the **Lion's Head Lighthouse** on Lion's Head Beach, and the **Cape Croker Lighthouse** at the tip of Cape Croker, a First Nations reserve. On Flowerpot Island in the Fathom Five National Marine Park, you can visit the **Flowerpot Island Light Station.** One of the most picturesque light stations is the **Killarney East Lighthouse,** on the bay near Killarney Provincial Park.

Today the lonely job of lighthouse keeper has generally gone the way of the dodo bird, as most lighthouse operations are automated. For a glimpse of old-fashioned lighthouse-keeping life, book a stay at **Cabot Head Lighthouse,** where you can spend a week as part of the assistant light keeper's program (late May-mid-Oct.). It's a working holiday where you help greet visitors to the lighthouse, assist in the gift shop, and pitch in with some housekeeping duties. For reservations or more information, complete the form on the **Friends of Cabot Head** website (www.cabothead.ca). The lighthouse stays are quite popular, so make plans well in advance.

interpretive programs, including guided hikes and children's activities. If you plan to camp on Flowerpot Island in the Fathom Five Marine Park, or to scuba-dive in any of the park territory, you must register at the Visitors Centre before heading out. The Visitors Centre is the northernmost point on the Bruce Trail. Check out the "sculpture" made from hikers' worn boots in the lobby and the **Bruce Trail Cairn** marking the end of the Bruce Trail. If you've hiked the entire trail, this is the spot to take your photo. Two hiking trails start at the center. It's an easy 800-meter (0.5-mile) walk to the **Little Dunks Bay Lookout.** The 4.8-kilometer (three-mile) **Burnt Point Loop Trail** meanders through the forest (with some rough, rocky patches) to Georgian Bay, where you can look out over the Fathom Five islands.

The Visitors Centre is a 10-minute walk from Tobermory's Little Tub Harbour along a flat, partly paved section of the Bruce Trail. By car, look for the park sign on Highway 6, just south of town.

Little Tub Harbour

Most of Tobermory's shops and services cluster around Little Tub Harbour. Boats to the Fathom Five islands leave from Little Tub, as do sightseeing cruises around Tobermory and the Fathom Five islands.

The two-hour Great Blue Heron glass bottom boat tour, run by **Blue Heron Tours** (519/596-2999, www.blueheronco.com, late June-early Sept., adults $36, seniors $34, ages 6-16 $27) on a 125-passenger ferry, sails to Big Tub Harbour, where you can see two 19th-century shipwrecks close to the surface, and continues around Russel Island, Cove Island, the Otter Islands, and Flowerpot Island. Another option, for the same price, is a two-hour sunset cruise (May-mid-Oct.). **Bruce Anchor Cruises** (519/596-2555 or 800/591-4254, www.bruceanchorcruises.com, adults $28, seniors $26, ages 6-16 $19) also offers two-hour tours that follow a similar route aboard a 47-passenger glass-bottom Zodiac.

Big Tub Harbour

Tobermory has a second port area, known as

Big Tub Harbour. The first lighthouse at Big Tub was constructed in 1885 to guide ships safely into port. The present-day **Big Tub Lighthouse,** a hexagonal tower that was automated in 1952, still performs that role at the harbor's mouth. The lighthouse isn't open to the public, but you can walk around the exterior and along the rocky shore. You can also swim or snorkel here.

The remains of two 19th-century ships lie in the shallow water of Big Tub Harbour. The *Sweepstakes,* a two-masted schooner, ran aground near Cove Island Lighthouse in 1885; the boat was towed to Big Tub Harbour, where it sank. The steamer *City of Grand Rapids* caught fire in 1907 while docked in Little Tub Harbour. The boat was towed out of the harbor to prevent the fire from spreading to other nearby ships; the burning ship then drifted into Big Tub Harbour and sank there.

You can see the shipwrecks on one of the boat tours out of Tobermory or on several of the Flowerpot Island boats. Snorkeling and scuba diving are allowed around the wrecks, but only at designated times, since boat traffic in the area can be heavy. Check with the **National Park Visitors Centre** (519/596-2233, www.pc.gc.ca) for details.

Entertainment and Shopping

Looking for a unique way to spend an evening? Storytellers and gregarious hosts Leslie Robbins-Conway and Paul Conway welcome visitors to their country home near Tobermory for **Voyageur Storytelling: Country Supper Storytelling Concerts** (56 Brinkman's Rd., Miller Lake, 519/795-7477, www.voyageurstorytelling.ca, 6pm-10:15pm Tues., Thurs., and Sat. mid-June-early Sept.; adults $46, seniors and students $42, children $36), pairing a multi-course home-cooked meal with a storytelling performance. Expect stories, poems, music, interesting conversation, and good fun.

At the annual **Orchid Festival** (www.orchidfest.ca, late May), you can join guided orchid-viewing walks, take flower drawing or photography workshops, or learn more about the peninsula's orchid population. Check the website for a schedule, or stop into festival headquarters at **National Park Visitors Centre** (120 Chi Sin Tib Dek Rd., Tobermory, 519/596-2233).

Most of the shops around Little Tub Harbour sell T-shirts and other ordinary souvenirs. One exception is **Circle Arts** (14 Bay St., 519/596-2541, www.circlearts.com, 10am-5:30pm daily mid-May-mid-Oct.), a fine-art

Big Tub Lighthouse, Tobermory

gallery showcasing prints, paintings, sculpture, photographs, jewelry, textiles, one-of-a-kind furniture, and other works crafted by Canadian artists, many of whom have ties to the Bruce Peninsula. You might find anything from a $15 ceramic candleholder to a $20,000 painting.

Accommodations

Motels and B&Bs cluster around, or within walking distance of, Little Tub Harbour. Other accommodations dot Highway 6 south of town; if you don't want to take your car everywhere, try to stay near the harbor. In July and August and on holiday weekends, even basic motel rooms go for over $100; it's a good idea to book in advance, or at least arrive early in the day. The **Tobermory Chamber of Commerce** website (www.tobermory.com) lists local accommodations with last-minute availability.

Inside this nondescript vinyl-sided house about a 15-minute walk from Little Tub Harbour is the surprisingly stylish **Molinari's B&B** (68 Harpur Dr., 877/596-1228, www.themolinaris.com, $125 d). Owners Maria and Bob, who relocated from Montreal after falling in love with the Bruce Peninsula during scuba-diving visits, decorated the three contemporary guest rooms in richly hued textiles and outfitted then with microwaves, fridges, coffeemakers, and small flat-screen TVs. Guests take breakfast in the sleek industrial kitchen; there's no other common space, though, so it's not a sit-around-and-chat kind of lodging.

The friendly **Blue Bay Motel** (32 Bay St., 519/596-2392, www.bluebay-motel.com, May-mid-Oct., $110-160 d), right above Little Tub Harbour, has 16 basic but comfortable rooms with fridges, coffeemakers, and updated linens; the best are the second-floor units with water views (the first-floor rooms face the parking lot). There's also a large three-bedroom suite with a full kitchen. You can borrow one of the motel bicycles to tool around the area.

The **Maple Golf Inn** (22 Maple Golf Crescent, 519/596-8166, www.maplegolfinn.ca, from $125 d, $200 suite), in a suburban home looking onto the Cornerstone Golf Club, is popular with hikers, since there's an access point to the Bruce Trail nearby. Hosts Jill and Lawrence Stewart serve a full breakfast to guests who stay in two comfortable main-floor rooms decorated in a modern country style, with quilts, wood floors, and private baths. Downstairs, a family-friendly basement suite, which sleeps up to five, has two bedrooms and a separate living room.

Looking for a true getaway? At ★ **E'Terra** (www.eterra.ca, $800-1,075 d), a sumptuous wood and stone manor hidden in the woods, the owners won't divulge the address until you make a reservation. Four of the six guest rooms are two-story suites, and all have French linens and heated flagstone floors. Guests can unwind in the spacious living room or in the cozy third-floor library and take a sauna or a dip in the saltwater pool. You could drive to Tobermory in just a few minutes, but why would you want to leave?

Food

Most of Tobermory's dining options are in or near Little Tub Harbour or along Highway 6. In a little house just south of town, **Little Tub Bakery** (4 Warner Bay Rd., at Hwy. 6, 519/596-8399, 9am-6pm Mon.-Fri. summer, call for off-season hours) is justifiably famous for their gooey butter tarts. The cinnamon rolls and freshly baked pies are also delicious. You can pick up a sandwich or homemade pizza for a picnic.

Surprised to find a vegetarian-friendly eatery on a golf course? **Ancient Cedars Café** (Cornerstone Golf Club, 7178 Hwy. 6, 519/596-8626, www.ancientcedarscafe.com, 9am-9pm Tues.-Sat. and 9am-4pm Sun.-Mon. summer, call for off-season hours, $8-12) does dish out burgers and steak sandwiches made from locally raised beef, but the menu also features vegan *bulgogi*, a barbecue seitan sandwich, and a tasty sweet potato and black bean burrito.

The owners of Molinari's B&B

operate **Molinari's Espresso Bar and Italian Restaurant** (53 Bay St., 519/596-1228, www.themolinaris.com, May-Oct.), cooking up breakfast, lunch, and dinner, including Italian sandwiches, salads, and pastas.

Several places in Tobermory serve fish-and-chips, but you can't miss the bright blue and yellow facade of **The Fish and Chip Place** (24 Bay St. S., 519/596-8380, www.the-fishandchipplace.com, lunch and dinner daily late May-mid-Oct., call for seasonal hours, $7-12). The small menu includes the eponymous whitefish and french fries; their fish taco won't put any Baja joints out of business, but this far north of the border, it will do. On a sunny afternoon, particularly if you've been hiking, a beer on the deck is a perfect reward.

Information and Services

The **Tobermory Chamber of Commerce Information Centre** (Hwy. 6, just south of Little Tub Harbour, 519/596-2452, www.to-bermory.com) can provide maps and information about attractions, lodging, and services. You can also park your car here for the day at no charge. **County of Bruce Tourism** (www.explorethebruce.com) has extensive information about Tobermory and the rest of the Bruce Peninsula.

The **Foodland Market** (9 Bay St., 519/596-2380, 7am-9pm daily) at Little Tub Harbour stocks basic supplies for picnics or camping and also has a coin laundry.

Getting There
CAR
Tobermory is approximately 300 kilometers (186 miles) northwest of Toronto, about a four-hour drive, weather and traffic permitting. Parking around Little Tub Harbour is restricted to two hours. If you're planning a longer stay in town, or heading out on a boat tour, leave your car in one of the free long-term parking lots. There's one at the Tobermory Chamber of Commerce Information Centre on Highway 6, two smaller lots on Head Street (between the Information Centre and Little Tub Harbour), and another on Legion Street, west of Highway 6.

BUS
Without a car, the most convenient way to travel from Toronto to Tobermory, Bruce Peninsula National Park, or other points on the peninsula is on the **Parkbus** (800/928-7101, www.parkbus.ca, one-way adults $60, seniors and students $54, ages 2-12 $30, round-trip adults $86, seniors and students

GEORGIAN BAY
THE BRUCE PENINSULA

freshly baked tarts from Little Tub Bakery

$77, ages 2-12 $43), which operates on selected weekends. The bus departs from several points in Toronto, including 30 Carlton Street (between Yonge St. and Church St., subway: College), and Dufferin Street at Bloor Street West (subway: Dufferin). On the Bruce Peninsula, the Parkbus drops off and picks up at stops in Wiarton, Lion's Head, the National Park's Cypress Lake campground, and Tobermory; check the website for details.

If you can't arrange your schedule to ride the Parkbus, the other bus option is to connect through Owen Sound. **Greyhound** (800/661-8747, www.greyhound.ca) can get you to Owen Sound from Toronto and points farther afield. From Owen Sound to Tobermory, **First Student Canada bus service** (2180 20th St. E., Owen Sound, 519/376-5712, www.tobermory.com, one-way adults $34, seniors and ages 4-12 $32) runs one bus a day in each direction Friday-Sunday and holiday Mondays July through early September. The schedule is timed to connect with the Manitoulin Island ferry.

FERRY
The **MS *Chi-Cheemaun* Ferry** (information 519/376-6601, reservations 800/265-3163, www.ontarioferries.com, mid-May-mid-Oct.), nicknamed "The Big Canoe," runs between Tobermory and South Baymouth on Manitoulin Island. The crossing takes about two hours, and the ship accommodates 638 passengers and 143 cars. The ferry cuts out several hours of driving time compared to the road route between Southern Ontario and Manitoulin. Reservations are advised, particularly if you're taking a car. The **Tobermory ferry terminal** is at 8 Eliza Street (519/596-2510).

Getting Around
Without a car, you can easily walk around Tobermory or to the National Park Visitors Centre, catch a boat to Flowerpot Island, and take other short hikes in the area. Some hotel or B&B owners will drop you at the trailhead for a day hike, so inquire when making

exploring The Grotto at Bruce Peninsula National Park

lodging reservations. **Thorncrest Outfitters** (7441 Hwy. 6, 519/596-8908, www.thorncrestoutfitters.com) runs a shuttle service for hikers or paddlers (they'll also transport your canoe or kayak) between Tobermory and Cyprus Lake, Dyer's Bay, or Lion's Head.

★ BRUCE PENINSULA NATIONAL PARK
Intricate rock formations. Caribbean-blue water. Centuries-old trees. Inland lakes. More than three dozen types of orchids. **Bruce Peninsula National Park** (www.pc.gc.ca, open year-round, $11.70 per vehicle), which encompasses 156 square kilometers (60 square miles) spread over several parcels of land, protects these natural features that are unique in Ontario. The park is at the northern tip of the Bruce Peninsula near the town of Tobermory.

The Grotto and Indian Head Cove
The park's most visited sights are the Grotto, a waterside cave, and the adjacent Indian

Head Cove, and with good reason. Through centuries of erosion, the waters of Georgian Bay have sculpted the area's soft limestone cliffs, leaving dramatic overhangs, carved rocks, and underwater caves, such as the Grotto. At Indian Head Cove, the rocks are sculpted into pillars, narrower at the bottom and wider at the top, resembling smaller versions of the "flowerpots" in the Fathom Five National Marine Park. Particularly on bright sunny days, the contrast between the brilliant blue-green bay, the polished white rocks along the shoreline, and the layered rock cliffs is striking.

You can climb down to sea level to explore the cave-like Grotto, but even if scrambling down steep rocks isn't your thing, you can still view the Grotto from above. At Indian Head Cove, the rock formations are on the pebbly beach, so no climbing is required. You can swim in Georgian Bay, although the water is cold year-round.

It's a moderate hike to the Grotto from the day-use parking area near the **Cyprus Lake Park Office** (Cyprus Lake Rd., off Hwy. 6, 519/596-2263), where several trails lead to Georgian Bay. Once at the shore, head north along the rocky shore to Indian Head Cove and then to the Grotto. Allow about 30-45 minutes to walk each way from the parking area. You must stop at the park office to pay a day-use parking fee ($11.70 per car) before you set out. There are restrooms at the Cyprus Lake office and near the Grotto, but no other services, so bring whatever food and water you need.

Cyprus Lake

From the Cyprus Lake day-use parking area (Cyprus Lake Rd., off Hwy. 6), you can walk down to the lake in just a few minutes. There's a sandy beach with somewhat warmer water than in chilly Georgian Bay, as well as picnic tables. The **Cyprus Lake Trail** follows the lakeshore. A mostly flat, 5.2-kilometer (3.2-mile) loop trail, it's a popular spot for bird-watching. Paddlers looking for a calm body of water to canoe or kayak can

head out into Cyprus Lake. In winter, you can snowshoe along Cyprus Lake and on to the Grotto. Park at the Cyprus Lake main gate, then follow the Cyprus Lake Trail to the Georgian Bay Trail.

There are no boat rentals at the lake, but in Tobermory, **Thorncrest Outfitters** (7441 Hwy. 6, 519/596-8908, www.thorncrestoutfitters.com) rents canoes and kayaks and can transport them to the lake. They also offer a number of full- and half-day guided paddling trips at various locations on the northern Bruce Peninsula.

★ The Bruce Trail

Serious hikers often plan their holidays to hike the **Bruce Trail** (www.brucetrail.org), doing sections of this 845-kilometer (525-mile) route in two-day, three-day, or week-long increments. They return to the trail until they've completed the entire route from the Niagara region to Tobermory. Yet you don't have to be an indomitable whole-trail hiker to enjoy the Bruce Trail. You can easily take day hikes along the trail, in and around Bruce Peninsula National Park.

From the Grotto, the Bruce Trail extends along Georgian Bay in both directions. If you continue to the west, you can hike all the way to Tobermory (18 kilometers, 11 miles). Between the Grotto and Little Cove (12.6 kilometers, 7.8 miles), the trail is quite difficult, with very rocky terrain, but you're rewarded with sweeping views of Georgian Bay. From Little Cove to Tobermory (5.4 kilometers, 3.4 miles), the trail flattens out and wends through the cedar forest.

Heading east from the Grotto along the bay, the Bruce Trail hugs the shore to Stormhaven (2.4 kilometers, 1.5 miles), where there's a primitive camping area and restroom. The trail then gets more difficult for the next 9.5 kilometers (six miles) to the High Dump camping area.

Because many sections of the Bruce Trail are quite rugged, get details about your route before you set out. The staff at the Cyprus Lake Park Office or the National Park Visitors

The Bruce Trail

One of Canada's iconic outdoor experiences is a hike along Ontario's Bruce Trail, an 845-kilometer (525-mile) hiking route that extends from the Niagara region to the tip of the Bruce Peninsula. How long does it take to complete the whole trail? If you hiked eight hours a day, covering about 30 kilometers (19 miles), it would take you roughly a month to hike end to end. However, unless you're an experienced hiker, this pace will likely be much too fast. And while some hikers do the entire trail straight through, far more end-to-end hikers complete the trail in a series of shorter excursions over several months or years.

Some sections of the trail are flat and easy, while others are quite rugged—get information about your route before you set out. A good source of trail information is the **Bruce Trail Conservatory** (905/529-6821 or 800/665-4453, www.brucetrail.org), a nonprofit committed to protecting and promoting the trail. They have a free online overview map, and you can download detailed maps of individual trail sections ($3 per map). If

The Bruce Trail runs from the Niagara region to the Bruce Peninsula.

you're serious about hiking the entire trail, consider purchasing the **Bruce Trail Reference** ($37), available on the conservatory website or through Canadian bookseller Chapters/Indigo (www.chapters.indigo.ca). Many Canadian libraries stock the guide, too. It's updated regularly—and there are changes and additions to the trail—so check for the most recent edition.

If you'd like to find hiking companions or join in group hikes, check out one of the nine Bruce Trail clubs, which help maintain the trail and arrange group activities in different regions. The **Peninsula Bruce Trail Club** (www.pbtc.ca) organizes hikes throughout the year on the Bruce Peninsula and publishes guides to peninsula day hikes. You can get a list of all the trail clubs from the Bruce Trail Conservatory website. The Bruce Trail Conservatory website includes a list of campgrounds that are accessible to the trail, as well as B&Bs and inns that welcome trail hikers. Many innkeepers whose lodgings are close to the trail will pick up or drop off hikers at nearby trailheads.

Another option for hikers who don't want to camp or lug gear is the **Home-to-Home B&B Network** (888/301-3224, www.hometohomenetwork.ca). Stay at any lodgings in this network of B&Bs, located between Wiarton and Tobermory, and hike to your next destination. The B&B owners will move your luggage to your next lodging. In the morning, you'll have a hot breakfast before beginning the day's hike. Reservations are required at least two weeks in advance.

Centre can help match a hike to your ability level.

Singing Sands Beach

On the west side of the peninsula, Singing Sands Beach (Dorcas Bay Rd.) looks like it's part of a completely different natural environment than the rocky eastern shores—and it is. The flat, sandy beach spreads out around Dorcas Bay with vistas out across Lake Huron;

it's a popular swimming spot. A short boardwalk trail loops around an adjacent marsh, and the three-kilometer (1.9-mile) **Forest Beach Loop Trail** is another easy walk that's good for bird-watching.

Camping

Within Bruce Peninsula National Park, **Cyprus Lake Campground** (Cyprus Lake Rd., mid-Apr.-mid-Oct. $23.40, mid-Oct.-Apr.

$15.70) has 232 drive-in campsites in three camping areas. All border Cyprus Lake and have restroom facilities with flush toilets and cold-water taps, but no showers. No electrical or sewer hookups are available. There are showers at Little Tub Harbour in Tobermory, about 15 kilometers (nine miles) north of Cyprus Lake. Ten furnished **yurts** (May-mid-Oct., $120), with outdoor propane barbecues, are available at Cyprus Lake. A central heated washroom with flush toilets and showers is located a short walk from the yurts. Between May and mid-October, you can reserve campsites and yurts through the Parks Canada Campground Reservation Service (877/737-3783, www.pccamping.ca). Reservations are advised, particularly during July and August. From mid-October to April, campsites are first-come, first-served.

Also in the park are two primitive backcountry campgrounds ($9.80 pp): **Stormhaven** and **High Dump.** Stormhaven is 2.4 kilometers (1.5 miles) east of the Grotto along Georgian Bay. High Dump is 9.5 kilometers (six miles) east of Stormhaven, or eight kilometers (five miles) from the parking area at Crane Lake (from Hwy. 6, take Dyer's Bay Rd. east to Crane Lake Rd.). To reach either area, you need to backpack in along the Bruce Trail. You must register at the Cyprus Lake Park Office (Cyprus Lake Rd., off Hwy. 6) before heading out. Between May and October, register by phone (519/596-2263) or in person at the office; the rest of the year, register at the self-service kiosk outside the office.

Stormhaven and High Dump each have nine sites with tent platforms and a composting toilet. No water is available, so bring your own or purify the water from the bay. Outside the park, the closest accommodations are in Tobermory.

Information and Services

For general information about Bruce Peninsula National Park, phone or visit the **National Park Visitors Centre** (120 Chi Sin Tib Dek Rd., Tobermory, 519/596-2233, www. pc.gc.ca). Between May and October, you can also contact the **Cyprus Lake Park Office** (Cyprus Lake Rd., off Hwy. 6, 519/596-2263).

★ FATHOM FIVE NATIONAL MARINE PARK

One of three national marine conservation areas in Canada, **Fathom Five National Marine Park** (519/596-2233, www.pc.gc.ca) includes 22 islands in Georgian Bay off the northern end of the Bruce Peninsula. Formed over 400 million years ago, these rocky islands are composed primarily of dolomite, a type of limestone. The main attractions for visitors are the distinctive rock formations known as "flowerpots." Narrow at the bottom and wider at the top, these rock stacks resemble massive stone pots. While the waves have slowly worn away the softer limestone on the pillars' lower end, the harder dolomite tops have survived, creating the unusual shape. Access to the park is by boat from the town of Tobermory.

More than 20 shipwrecks lie within the park's territory, making it a popular destination for scuba divers. In fact, the park gets its name from William Shakespeare's play *The Tempest,* in which the following lines describe the father of Ferdinand, who is feared dead in a shipwreck:

Full fathom five thy father lies;

Of his bones are coral made;

Those are pearls that were his eyes:

Nothing of him that doth fade

But doth suffer a sea-change

Into something rich and strange.

Sea-nymphs hourly ring his knell

Hark! now I hear them, ding-dong, bell.

A fathom is a unit of measure roughly equal to 1.8 meters (six feet), so "fathom five" is nine meters, or about 30 feet—a long way down!

Scuba Diving and Snorkeling

While you might not think of such a northern location as a prime scuba destination, Fathom Five has some of the world's best freshwater diving. Not only is the water generally clear, but the combination of underwater cliffs, caves, and other geological formations, along with the more than 20 shipwrecks in the area, give divers plenty to explore.

All divers must register in person in Tobermory at the **National Park Visitors Centre** (120 Chi Sin Tib Dek Rd., 519/596-2233, www.pc.gc.ca, national park admission fee adults $5.80, seniors $4.90, children $2.90). The park charges divers a daily fee of $4.90 pp in addition to the park admission fee and the cost of boat transportation. If you're planning to dive at least four days, buy an annual divers' pass ($19.60).

Several companies in Tobermory run single-day and multiday dive trips to the Fathom Five islands and surrounding areas. They also offer scuba lessons and gear rentals. Contact **Divers Den** (3 Bay St., 519/596-2363, www.diversden.ca), **G+S Watersports** (8 Bay St. S., 519/596-2200, www.gswatersports.net),

or **Tobermory Aquasports** (7037 Hwy. 6, 519/596-8474, www.tobermoryaquasports.com). While not all the shipwrecks are visible to snorkelers, some are, and you'll see them much more clearly than you would from a glass-bottom boat. Divers Den offers two-hour (adults $52, kids $28, families $135) and four-hour (adults $64, kids $32, families $72) snorkeling tours; they provide guidance, snorkeling gear, and the thick warm wetsuits you'll need to swim in the chilly water. G+S Watersports runs similar snorkeling excursions.

Flowerpot Island

Unless you have your own boat, only one of the park's 22 islands is accessible to visitors: Flowerpot Island, named for the two towering rock pillars known as the "flowerpots." These rock stacks sit waterside on the island's eastern shore.

Tour boats from Tobermory dock at Beachy Cove on the east side of Flowerpot Island. The island isn't large, at about two square kilometers (0.77 square miles), so it's only about a 15-minute walk from Beachy Cove to the first **small flowerpot,** which is seven meters (23 feet) high, and a few minutes farther to the **large flowerpot,** which stands 12 meters

snorkeling for shipwrecks off the Bruce Peninsula

(40 feet) high. From the flowerpots, you can follow the **Loop Trail,** passing a small cave. The path up to the cave is easy to miss; it's on the left just beyond the flowerpots. You can't go inside the cave, but you can peer into the entrance.

Beyond the cave, the Loop Trail continues to the **Flowerpot Island Light Station** on the island's northeast tip. The first lighthouse on the island went into service in 1897; in the 1960s, the original light was replaced with a steel lighthouse tower that's still flashing its beacon today. You can walk out to the tower and to an adjacent observation deck with a view across Georgian Bay. Near the light station is the light keeper's house, which contains a small museum (July-Aug.).

To return to Beachy Cove from the lighthouse, either backtrack along the trail past the flowerpots or continue on the Loop Trail up and over the bluffs in the middle of the island. This latter section of the Loop Trail is more rugged; park staff advise allowing at least an extra hour to return via this route.

If you can tolerate cold water (or wear a wetsuit), you can swim or snorkel off Flowerpot Island. The beaches are rocky, so wear protective footwear. The best swimming spots are near Beachy Cove or around the flowerpots. In either location, be alert for boat traffic.

CAMPING

Camping is your only option if you want to spend the night on Flowerpot Island. The park accepts **camping reservations** (519/596-2233, ext. 221) each year beginning in early May. The **Flowerpot Island Campground** ($9.80 pp) has six basic tent sites, all a stone's throw from the shore and a 5- to 10-minute walk from the Beachy Cove boat dock. There's a composting toilet nearby but no showers or running water. Bring your own water or purify the bay water for drinking. No supplies are available on the island. Parks Canada cautions that campers should bring enough food, water, and warm clothing to last extra days,

since boat service back to the mainland can be canceled if the weather turns bad.

INFORMATION AND SERVICES

Park staff are frequently on duty at Flowerpot Island's Beachy Cove during the summer. Otherwise, get information at the **National Park Visitors Centre** (120 Chi Sin Tib Dek Rd., 519/596-2233, www.pc.gc.ca, 9am-5pm Sun.-Mon. and Thurs.-Fri., 8am-5pm Sat. mid-May-late June, 8am-8pm daily late June-early Sept., 9am-5pm Thurs.-Mon. early Sept.-mid-Oct.) before you leave Tobermory.

A small volunteer-run snack bar near the lighthouse is open during the summer, but hours are erratic. There are restrooms at Beachy Cove between the ferry dock and the campground, and near the lighthouse. It's almost worth hiking to the light station just to use the **Loo with a View,** with its vistas across the bay.

GETTING THERE

The national park does not run its own boats; instead, it works with two private companies that offer boat trips to Flowerpot Island from mid-May to mid-October. Sailing schedules vary seasonally, so check their websites or phone for details. Also confirm when the last boats leave Flowerpot Island to return to the mainland, and get back to the dock at Beachy Cove in plenty of time. You don't want an unexpected overnight stay!

Both **Blue Heron Tours** (Little Tub Harbour, 519/596-2999, www.blueheronco. com) and **Bruce Anchor Cruises** (519/596-2555 or 800/591-4254, www.bruceanchor-cruises.com) run boats from Little Tub Harbour to Beachy Cove and offer these island shuttles combined with shipwreck-viewing tours. If you just want to get to Flowerpot Island, Blue Heron's jet boat (round-trip adults $34, seniors $32, ages 6-16 $25) shuttles you between Little Tub Harbour and Beachy Cove in 15 minutes. For a few dollars more, you can add a brief ride through Big Tub Harbour to look at the remains of two shipwrecks on the 25-minute island shuttle and shipwrecks tour (round-trip adults $40, seniors $37, ages 6-16 $30). You don't see much—the wrecks look like shadows under the water—but it's as close as you can get to the sunken ships without snorkeling or scuba diving. You can see the shipwrecks more clearly on the glass bottom boat tour (adults $40, seniors $37, ages 6-16 $30) en route to Flowerpot Island. Bruce Anchor Cruises can also take you to Flowerpot Island with stops to view the shipwrecks (adults $37, seniors $35, ages 6-16 $29). They operate different boats with varying schedules, so check to see what's most convenient for you.

You must pay the national park admission fee (adults $5.80, seniors $4.90, children $2.90) in addition to the price for the boat trips. Park admission includes access to Flowerpot Island and to the National Park Visitors Centre in Tobermory.

DYER'S BAY

Unlike many of the Bruce Peninsula's lighthouses, which you can see only from the exterior, at the **Cabot Head Lighthouse** (806 Cabot Head Rd., Miller Lake, 519/795-7780, www.cabothead.ca, 10am-7pm daily late May-mid-Oct., donation $3), you can venture inside. The lower levels of the red-and-white wooden structure are a museum with exhibits about local marine history. Climb up to the observation tower for a light keeper's view out across the bay. The original Cabot Head Lighthouse began operation in 1896. It remained in use until 1968, when it was torn down and replaced with the current light, which is an automated beacon. The lighthouse is about 40 kilometers (25 miles) southeast of Tobermory, about a 45-minute drive. From Highway 6, go east on Dyer's Bay Road.

LION'S HEAD

Lion's Head is a friendly little village on Georgian Bay in the approximate north-south midpoint of the Bruce Peninsula. You can stroll or swim at the beach, browse the village shops, or have a beer in the local pub. With its central location, Lion's Head is a convenient base for exploring the peninsula, particularly if you want to visit sights beyond the Tobermory area.

Set on the bay at the mouth of Lion's Head harbor, **Lion's Head Lighthouse** is a re-creation of the original light station built here in 1903. Students at the local high school constructed the current lighthouse in 1983, using plans for the original structure. The lighthouse is particularly photogenic, with the

Lion's Head Lighthouse

bay and the cliffs of the Niagara Escarpment as a backdrop.

On the south side of town, **Lion's Head Provincial Park** (519/389-9056, www.ontarioparks.com, free) is known for its "potholes," deep, cylindrical holes carved by erosion into the limestone rocks. It's about a 20-minute walk along a flat section of the Bruce Trail to two of the large potholes. The trail continues toward Georgian Bay, where it becomes more difficult as it hugs the cliffs. The reward for the climb up and along the tops of the rocks is a spectacular view of the cliffs and the bay. This section of the trail isn't recommended for small children, as the trail veers quite close to the cliffs. Access to the potholes trail is from Moore Street; the trail starts opposite 128 Moore Street. The park has no restrooms or other services.

The **Central Bruce Peninsula Chamber Of Commerce** (2866 Hwy. 6, Ferndale, 519/793-3178, www.centralbrucepeninsula.ca, daily July-Aug., Sat.-Sun. mid-May-June and Sept.-mid-Oct.) runs a seasonal visitor information center on Highway 6 at Highway 9 (the Lion's Head turnoff). The rest of the year, staff answer questions by phone. Lion's Head is about 250 kilometers (160 miles) north of Toronto. There's no public transportation to or around the area.

Accommodations and Food

Big rooms, a beachside location, reasonable rates, and a warm welcome from owner Barbara Grison and her staff are the reasons to stay at the **Lion's Head Beach Motel and Cottages** (1 McNeil St., 519/793-3155, www.lionsheadbeachmotelandcottages.ca, $89-115 s, $105-125 d). Although the family-friendly motel rooms won't win any design prizes, they're well maintained, larger than average, and include kitchenettes. The newer two- and three-bedroom cottages ($125-260) would be even more comfortable if you've brought Grandma or the kids.

If you're not a regular at **The Lion's Head Inn & Restaurant** (8 Helen St., 519/793-4601, www.lionsheadinn.ca, 11am-11pm daily May-Oct., 4pm-9pm Wed.-Sat. Nov.-Apr., $10-20), you may feel like one after you've stopped for a beer in this convivial pub. The food is a notch above basic bar grub and includes burgers, pasta, fish-and-chips, and steaks. Built as a boardinghouse in 1879, the inn has three simple guest rooms upstairs ($80-120 d), two with a shared bath and one with a private bath.

In the center of Lion's Head village, **Marydale's Restaurant** (76 Main St., 519/793-4224, 8am-8pm daily summer, 8am-7pm daily fall-spring, $7-15) serves substantial breakfasts and simple home-style fare year-round.

It's worth visiting the small **Lion's Head Farmers Market** (1 Forbes St., 9am-noon Sat. late May-mid-Oct.) just for its open-air setting right on Lion's Head Beach. Vendors sell produce, muffins, other baked goods, and crafts. Pull off Highway 6 at the **Harvest Moon Organic Bakery** (3927 Hwy. 6, 519/592-5742, www.harvestmoonbakery.ca, 9am-4:30pm Wed.-Sun. July-Aug., 9am-4:30pm Thurs.-Sun. May-June and Sept.-Oct.) for butter tarts, hearty potato-filled pasties, or homemade multigrain bread. Besides sampling the treats that come out of this riotously colorful little house, you can stroll around the quirky sculpture garden (free). The bakery is about 10 minutes north of Ferndale, on the west side of the highway.

WIARTON AND VICINITY

Wiarton sits on Colpoys Bay, an inlet off Georgian Bay, with the cliffs of the Niagara Escarpment towering above the water. Highway 6, the peninsula's main north-south route, runs straight through town, where it's called Berford Street. While its year-round population is under 2,500, Wiarton has all the basic services you need, including a 24-hour grocery store. Many of Wiarton's limestone or brick buildings downtown date to the mid-1800s; the village was incorporated in 1880, and the railroad reached the area the following year. The former railroad station is now the town's information center.

Two fingers of land jutting into Georgian Bay on either side of Wiarton are worth exploring. To the north, Cape Crocker is a First Nations reserve; to the east, you can head toward the village of Big Bay, visiting caves, gardens, and an ice cream shop en route. Wiarton's most famous resident may be **Wiarton Willie,** a weather-forecasting groundhog. Similar to the American Punxsutawney Phil, Wiarton Willie comes out of his burrow annually on Groundhog Day (Feb. 2). If he sees his shadow, Canada's winter will last another six weeks; if he doesn't, spring is supposedly on the way. For much of the year, you can view Willie in his pen outside the Wiarton branch of the Bruce County Public Library (578 Brown St., at William St.). Local sculptor Dave Robinson crafted a 4.5-ton limestone statue of the town's notable groundhog. *Willie Emerging* sits near the beach in **Bluewater Park** (William St.). Also in the park is Wiarton's former train station, an ornate wooden building built in 1904 and moved to its present site in 1971.

East of Wiarton, in the hamlet of Big Bay, you can stroll among the irises, lilacs, poppies, and lavender in the peaceful privately owned **Kepplecroft Gardens** (504156 Grey Rd. 1, Big Bay, 519/534-1090, www.keppelcroft. com, 10am-5pm Wed.-Sun. May-mid-Oct., donation $3). With a Zen garden, a woodland garden, and rock sculptures, Kepplecroft Gardens are part of a regional network of private gardens, known as the **Rural Gardens of Grey and Bruce Counties** (www.ruralgardens.ca), that are open to visitors. The website lists gardens hours and locations; you can also pick up a *Rural Gardens* map at any of the information centers on the Bruce Peninsula.

Wiarton celebrates its weather-forecasting groundhog during the annual **Wiarton Willie Festival** (519/534-5492, www.wiartonwillie.com), a winter carnival that includes a parade, fireworks, concerts, pancake breakfasts, sleigh rides, and, of course, Willie's prediction for the end of winter. The festival takes place for several days around Groundhog Day (Feb. 2).

Stop into the **Wiarton Information Centre** (Bluewater Park, 519/534-3111, www. visitwiarton.ca, May-early Sept.) in the former train station. You can also get visitor information from the **Town of South Bruce Peninsula** (315 George St., 519/534-1400 or 877/534-1400, www.southbrucepeninsula.com, 8:30am-4:30pm Mon.-Fri.), or the **County of Bruce Tourism** (578 Brown St., 519/534-5344 or 800/268-3838, www.explorethebruce.com). Wiarton is about 220 kilometers (137 miles) northwest of Toronto. There's no public transportation in the area, so it's difficult to explore without a car.

Cape Croker

Part of the Saugeen Ojibway First Nations territory, the 6,000-hectare (14,825-acre) Cape Croker Peninsula juts out into Georgian Bay north of Wiarton. The peninsula's Ojibwa name, Neyaashiinigmiing, means "a point of land nearly surrounded by water," and the name is apt—except for a sliver of land connecting the peninsula to the mainland, it's ringed by the waters of the bay. Cape Croker is a pretty spot for a drive or hike, particularly on the north side of the peninsula with views across the water to the limestone bluffs of the Niagara Escarpment. You can drive out to the **Cape Croker Lighthouse,** built in 1902 on the tip of the cape, but the interior isn't open to the public, and the setting, behind a chain-link fence, isn't that picturesque.

Near the mainland end of the peninsula, the **Cape Croker Indian Park** (519/534-0571, www.capecrokerpark.com, $10 per vehicle) has a lovely beach and hiking trails as well as a campground. The park is also the site of the annual **Cape Croker Powwow** (www. nawash.ca, late Aug., $5), where you can experience the music, dance, and other traditions of the local First Nations community. Visitors are welcome at the powwow as long as they are respectful of local customs. Ask permission before taking photos or videos, and leave the beer at home—the powwow is an alcohol-free event.

Accommodations and Food

In the late 1990s, Evan LeBlanc and Dave Peebles bought a basic roadside motel overlooking Colpoys Bay, and they've steadily upgraded the property that is now the three-story **Waterview on the Bay** (501205 Island View Dr., 519/534-0921 or 877/534-0921, www.waterview.ca, Apr.-Oct., $100-160 d). The 21 rooms include simple rooms with two double beds and a fridge and the "luxury suites," with whirlpool tubs, sleigh beds, and expansive bay views. Also on the property are five two- or three-bedroom cottages ($200-250). There's a swimming pool and a sandy beach. The Waterview is family-friendly, pet-friendly, and just overall friendly.

Bonnie Howe and Phil Howard purchased a farm east of Wiarton and opened **Longlane Bed & Breakfast** (483078 Colpoy's Range Rd., 519/534-3901, www.longlane.ca, $90 s, $110 d), where they raise cattle and chickens and grow their own vegetables. Upstairs in the 1902 farmhouse, the three guest rooms are decorated with quilts and country curtains. Guests share two baths, as well as a sitting area with a TV, and in the morning, they tuck into hearty farm breakfasts around the communal kitchen table. The owners will shuttle hikers to the Bruce Trail nearby.

Wiarton's best restaurant, the **Green Door Café** (563 Berford St., 510/534-3278, www.thegreendoorcafe.com, 11am-3pm Sun.-Tues., 11am-8pm Wed.-Sat. late June-Aug., 11am-3pm Sun.-Wed., 11am-8pm Thurs.-Sat. Sept.-late June, $5-14) looks like a small-town coffee shop, where local retirees stop in for cups of joe and grilled cheese sandwiches. At this unassuming eatery, though, the straightforward sandwiches and hearty main dishes are well prepared from fresh ingredients. Try the delicious, garlicky Caesar salad or the meaty cabbage rolls.

Tiny **Big Bay General Store** (250854 Big Bay Sideroad at Grey Rd. 1, 519/534-4523, daily late May-early Sept., Sat.-Sun. spring and fall), east of Wiarton, doesn't stock many groceries, but they do serve delicious homemade ice cream. They make more than 80 different flavors, with 10 to 12 available at a time. Call to confirm open hours before making a special trip.

CAMPING

Owned and operated by the Chippewas of Nawash First Nation, the **Cape Croker Indian Park** (519/534-0571, www.capecrokerpark.com, early May-mid-Oct., $29-39) has an enviable waterfront location on Sydney Bay. The 210-hectare (520-acre) property has 315 campsites with showers, flush toilets, laundry facilities, a swimming beach, and canoe rentals. Prime waterfront sites look across to the cliffs of the Niagara Escarpment, while other sites are tucked into the woods. A small camping cabin with two bunks ($65) is also available. Definitely reserve in advance for the August powwow, and you may want to book ahead for the popular waterfront sites, for the cabin, or for holiday weekend stays.

SAUBLE BEACH

On Lake Huron at the south end of the Bruce Peninsula, Sauble Beach is a full-fledged beach-holiday town. This sun-and-fun community has burger stands and soft-serve ice cream shops, T-shirt sellers and bikini boutiques, and, oh, yes, a sandy lakeshore beach that seems to go on and on. The world's second-longest freshwater beach, Sauble Beach (Lakeshore Dr.) is a flat paradise of sand that extends for 11 kilometers (nearly seven miles); only Wasaga Beach, east of Collingwood, is longer. The early French explorers who traversed this area named it La Rivière au Sable ("River to the Sand") for the nearby Sauble River, but by the end of the 19th-century, the town was known as Sauble Beach for its major geographical asset.

Since the water is fairly shallow, Sauble Beach is a good choice for families with younger kids. The atmosphere in July and August can be rather honky-tonk, but the farther you go from the heart of town, the easier it is to find a peaceful spot to lay your towel. And despite the summer crowds, the beach is undeniably beautiful, and sunsets over the lake can be spectacular. Outside summer high season, you'll sometimes have the fine golden sand almost to yourself. Beach parking is available in lots right on the sand and along Lakeshore Road. Prepare for epic summer traffic jams. The **Sauble Beach Sandfest** (Lakeshore Blvd., www.saublebeach.com) takes place the first weekend of August and turns the beach into a giant outdoor sand sculpture gallery, drawing both professional and amateur sand sculptors.

Sauble Beach has a large assortment of standard beach motels and cottages. The **Sauble Beach Information Centre** (672 Main St., 519/422-1262, www.saublebeach. com, 9am-5pm Mon.-Fri., 10am-3pm Sat.) has information about cottage rentals and lists of area accommodations. If you prefer a more peaceful atmosphere, you could stay in Wiarton, about 20 kilometers (12.5 miles) from Sauble Beach, and come to the beach during the day. Restaurants in town, which are clustered along Main Street and on 2nd Avenue North (one block east of the beach), tend to serve burgers, pizza, and other eat-and-run fare.

Sauble Beach is about 220 kilometers (137 miles) northwest of Toronto via Highways 6/10. After you pass through Owen Sound, continue on Highway 6 to Bruce Road 8, which heads west into Sauble Beach.

Sauble Falls Provincial Park

About one kilometer (0.6 miles) north of Sauble Beach, the small provincial **Sauble Falls Provincial Park** (Sauble Falls Pkwy./ County Rd. 13, 519/422-1952, www.ontarioparks.com, late Apr.-Oct., $14.50 per vehicle) couldn't feel more different than the frenzied tourist crush of the nearby town. Although it does get busy in summer, it still feels like an escape into the woods.

The petite waterfalls along the Sauble River that give the park its name descend in tiers, almost like an aquatic wedding cake, over a staircase of dolomite limestone. You can watch the falls from a small viewing platform or along either side of the river; it's a lovely spot for a picnic. In spring and fall, you may see salmon and rainbow trout attempting to swim upstream over each ledge of the falls. You can also go canoeing or kayaking on a stretch of the Sauble River that winds through the park. Canoe and kayak rentals (daily mid-June-early Sept., Sat.-Sun. early Sept.-mid-Oct., call for fall hours) are available off Sauble Falls Parkway just north of the river.

Sauble Falls Provincial Park

Sauble Falls Provincial Park has 152 campsites (tent sites $35-40, electrical sites $40-46). In both the East Campground and the larger, radio-free West Campground, the nicest sites front the Sauble River. Both areas have flush toilets and showers; the West Campground has laundry facilities. Reserve campsites up to five months in advance though the **Ontario Parks Reservations Service** (888/668-7275, www.ontarioparks.com, reservation fee online $11, by phone $13).

OWEN SOUND

It's hard to imagine that this small community of about 22,000 was once known as "Chicago of the North." From 1885 through 1912, when the Canadian Pacific Railway (CPR) made Owen Sound the terminus of its steamship line, the town's port was the busiest in the upper Great Lakes. Many of the town's Victorian homes and buildings date to this era. Alas, in 1912, the Canadian Pacific Railway moved its shipping operations farther east to Port McNicoll, Ontario, which had better rail connections, thus ending Owen Sound's glory years.

For a small city, Owen Sound has a large number of museums and historic attractions. To stroll through the town's history, pick up the *Historic Downtown Walking Tour* brochure at the **Owen Sound Tourist Information Centre** (1155 1st Ave. W., 519/371-9833, www.owensound.ca). Many grand homes, built in the late 1800s, are along 1st Avenue West, while Victorian-era commercial buildings still stand along 2nd Avenue East.

Owen Sound was a destination for formerly enslaved people who came north along the Underground Railroad. To learn about this heritage, follow two self-guided tours of sites that were important to African Canadians. Pick up brochures about these tours—*The Freedom Trail,* a 10-kilometer (six-mile) walking or cycling tour, and the *Owen Sound Underground Railroad Driving Tour*—at the **Owen Sound Tourist Information Centre**

(1155 1st Ave. W., 519/371-9833, www.owensound.ca) or on the website.

Grey Roots Museum and Archives

If you think that a museum about a region's roots is a musty trove of papers and old tools, think again. The contemporary **Grey Roots Museum and Archives** (102599 Grey Rd. 18, 519/376-3690 or 877/473-9766, www.greyroots.com, 10am-5pm daily late May-mid-Oct., 10am-5pm Tues.-Sat. mid-Oct.-late May, adults $8, seniors $6, ages 5-12 $4, families $20) showcases the history and culture of Owen Sound and the surrounding region with cool multimedia features that include films, radio stories, and computer-based displays.

Start in the Grey County gallery, where the permanent "Grey Roots" exhibit introduces you to the people who settled the region—from the local First Nations to early pioneers to notable citizens such as Agnes Macphail, a Grey County native who became Canada's first woman elected to Parliament. Other galleries host temporary and traveling exhibitions; recent exhibits have focused on "Saints and Sinners" (how alcohol influenced Grey County's development), letters between local soldiers and their families during the Great War (World War I), and Victorian-era death and mourning customs.

If you have kids in tow, explore **Moreston Heritage Village** (11am-4:30pm daily June-early Sept.), the on-site pioneer village that's staffed by costumed volunteers. Watch the blacksmith at work, visit the 1850s log cabin, or check out the schoolhouse. The museum is located about seven kilometers (4.4 miles) south of downtown.

Tom Thomson Art Gallery

Artist Tom Thomson (1877-1917) grew up outside Owen Sound in the town of Leith. A member of the Group of Seven—notable Canadian landscape artists of the early 20th century—Thomson is best known for the paintings he created in Algonquin Park between 1912 and 1917, until his death, reportedly by drowning, in Algonquin's Canoe Lake. The small, modern **Tom Thomson Art Gallery** (840 1st Ave. W., 519/376-1932, www.tomthomson.org, 10am-5pm Mon.-Sat., noon-5pm Sun. late May-mid-Oct., 11am-5pm Tues.-Fri., noon-5 Sat.-Sun. mid-Oct.-late May, donation $5) mounts changing exhibits of work by Thomson and other Ontario artists.

Billy Bishop Home and Museum

Owen Sound native William Avery Bishop (1894-1956), a fighter pilot with the British Royal Flying Corps, became one of the most decorated Canadians serving in World War I. Bishop's childhood home, in a restored Victorian mansion, is now the **Billy Bishop Home and Museum** (948 3rd Ave. W., 519/371-0031, www.billybishop.org, 10am-5pm Mon.-Sat., noon-5pm Sun. late May-mid-Oct., 11am-5pm Tues.-Fri., noon-5 Sat.-Sun. mid-Oct.-late May, donation $5) that includes artifacts from Bishop's life and from World Wars I and II, with an emphasis on aviation history.

Owen Sound Marine and Rail Museum

Located in Owen Sound's former Canadian National Railway station (the station's waiting room now houses the Owen Sound Tourist Information Centre), the **Owen Sound Marine and Rail Museum** (1155 1st Ave. W., 519/371-3333, 10am-5pm Mon.-Sat., noon-5pm Sun. late May-mid-Oct., call for off-season hours, donation) commemorates the region's glory days as a ship and rail hub in the late 1800s. There are ship models and railroad exhibits; outside, you can climb on board a restored caboose.

Harrison Park and the Black History Cairn

Owen Sound was one of the northernmost stops on the Underground Railroad, the network of safe houses that protected

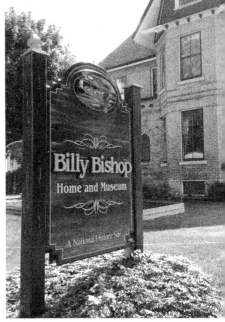

Canadian aviator Billy Bishop grew up in this Owen Sound home.

slaves fleeing from the United States in the 1800s.

The **Black History Cairn** (www.owensound.ca), located in **Harrison Park** (2nd Ave. E.), memorializes the journey of enslaved people into the north. This outdoor sculpture includes eight tiles inlaid in the ground, incorporating quilt patterns that represented coded messages to escaping slaves—according to legend, the patterns were originally sewn into quilts. One pattern symbolizes the North Star, which guided slaves to freedom; a log cabin symbol indicates a safe house; another is a sailboat, signifying a water crossing. Around the tiles is a stone structure representing the ruins of a church, with windows looking toward the Sydenham River. According to Bonita Johnson de Matteis, the artist who designed the cairn, newly freed people might have looked out similar church windows in Owen Sound as they gave thanks for their freedom. Johnson de Matteis herself is a descendent of a slave who escaped from the United States and settled in Owen Sound.

Harrison Park is located off 2nd Avenue East, south of downtown. Once you arrive in Harrison Park, to find the Black History Cairn, walk north from the parking area near the Harrison Park Inn; the cairn is just past the playground. The park is a lovely spot for a picnic, and it's crisscrossed with trails for hiking, running, and cycling; it also has three playgrounds, as well as canoe rentals.

Coffin Ridge Boutique Winery

In the rolling hills east of town, with views to Georgian Bay, the small-batch **Coffin Ridge Boutique Winery** (599448 2nd Concession N., Annan, 519/371-9565, www.coffinridge.ca, 11am-6pm Mon.-Sat., 11am-5pm Sun. summer, call or check the website for off-season hours) cultivates 10 hectares (25 acres) of cold-climate grapes that are made into drinkable one-of-a-kind wines. Sample what's on offer at the tasting bar, or have a glass with a cheese and charcuterie plate overlooking the vineyard. In the restroom, videos of *The Munsters,* the quirky 1960s TV monster show, play up the coffin theme.

Entertainment and Shopping

The historic downtown **Roxy Theatre** (251 9th St. E., 519/371-2833 or 888/446-7699, www.roxytheatre.ca), built in 1912, hosts live theater and musical performances throughout the year.

The first weekend in August, Owen Sound's annual **Emancipation Celebration Festival** (Harrison Park, 2nd Ave. E., www.emancipation.ca) recalls the struggles of the formerly enslaved people who traveled the Underground Railroad to freedom in Canada. First held in 1862, it's the longest continuously running emancipation festival in North America. Events include a speaker's forum, music, and a picnic.

From photography to metalwork to jewelry, the **Owen Sound Artists' Co-op** (279 10th St. E., 519/371-0479, www.osartistsco-op.com, 9:30am-5:30pm Mon.-Sat.) displays and sells the work of its roughly 40 member artists, all from the local area.

Accommodations

Owen Sound's lodging options range from chain motels (primarily along Highway 6/10 on the town's east side) to Victorian-style bed-and-breakfasts.

The most romantic inn in town is the ★ **Highland Manor** (867 4th Ave. A W., 519/372-2699 or 877/372-2699, www.highlandmanor.ca, no children under 14, $120 s, $170 d), a grand brick mansion on a shady residential street. Guests can browse books about the area in the library and take their elaborate breakfasts in the formal dining room. Upstairs, the guest rooms have working fireplaces and antique furnishings. Owners Linda Bradford and Paul Neville are passionate about local history, and they're a wealth of information about things to do nearby.

In a circa-1900 Victorian home, **MacLean Estate Bed & Breakfast** (404 9th St. E., 519/416-5326, www.macleanestate.com, $109-129 d) retains period details like original leaded-glass windows and pocket doors, but there's nothing stuffy about the welcome you get from owners Jamie Heimbecker and Matthew MacLean, who've updated the B&B with air-conditioning, HDTV, DVD players, and fast Wi-Fi. The largest of the second-floor guest rooms has a turret and a private bath; the other two share a large bath. Staying here includes a full breakfast and lots of local tips; Jamie grew up nearby and is tapped into the local community.

Although it's out of the town center on a charmless stretch of road, and most of its 100 rooms are standard chain accommodations, the **Best Western Inn on the Bay** (1800 2nd Ave. E., 519/371-9200 or 800/780-7234, www.bestwesternontario.com, $140-240 d) does have rooms overlooking Georgian Bay and a hot tub facing the waterfront.

Food

If you'd like to wander and check out food options, head downtown to 2nd Avenue East, between 10th and 7th Streets. The year-round **Owen Sound Farmers Market** (114 8th St. E., 519/371-3433, www.owensoundfarmersmarket.ca, 8am-12:30pm Sat.) sells baked goods, crafts, and seasonal produce.

Ginger Press Bookshop and Café (848 2nd Ave. E., 519/376-4233, www.gingerpress.com, bookshop 9:30am-6pm Mon.-Fri., 9am-2pm Sat., café 9:30am-2pm Mon.-Fri., 9am-noon Sat., $5-12) is part bookstore and part casual café, serving soup, sandwiches, and other light meals. Fresh-pressed apple ginger juice is their specialty. Wi-Fi is free.

At the eclectic **Kathmandu Café** (941 2nd Ave. E., 519/374-0500, www.kathmanducafe.ca, generally 11am-9pm Mon.-Sat., call to confirm hours, $15-25), local ingredients join Asian and global influences to create curries and other world-beat dishes.

Named in homage to Norma Jeane Mortenson, better known as the actress Marilyn Monroe, **Norma Jean's Bistro** (243 8th St. E., 519/376-2232, 11:30am-10pm Mon.-Sat., $12-27) has been a downtown fixture since 1984. Though the menu looks fairly standard—pastas, sandwiches, chicken, steak—the creative kitchen livens things up with seasonal ingredients and as many surprising twists as a Hollywood flick.

Information and Services

The **Owen Sound Tourist Information Centre** (1155 1st Ave. W., 519/371-9833 or 888/675-5555, www.owensound.ca), which shares a building with the Marine and Rail Museum, is full of information about attractions and lodgings around town. The regional tourism association, **Grey County Tourism** (102599 Grey Rd. 18, 519/376-3265 or 877/733-4739, www.visitgrey.ca), has a helpful information desk in the lobby of the Grey Roots Museum.

Getting There and Around

Owen Sound is 190 kilometers (120 miles) northwest of Toronto, about a 2.5-hour drive via Highways 6 and 10. **Greyhound Bus Lines** (City Transit Centre, 1020 3rd Ave. E., 519/376-5375 or 800/661-8747, www.greyhound.ca) runs one direct bus daily in each direction between Toronto and Owen Sound (about 4 hours, $36-59 pp). The **Grey Bruce Airbus** (800/361-0393, www.greybruceairbus.com, adults $75 one-way, $136 round-trip) operates four trips daily in each direction between Toronto's Pearson Airport and the Owen Sound Days Inn (950 6th St. E.).

The majority of Owen Sound's roadways are numbered streets and avenues (streets run east-west, avenues run north-south). The Sydenham River divides the east and west sides, so a "west" address, such as the Tom Thomson Gallery on 1st Avenue West, is west of the river, while an "east" address is east of the river.

Owen Sound's attractions are clustered in two main areas—around downtown and south of the center. The main downtown shopping street is 2nd Avenue East, south of 10th Street and east of the river. From downtown, you can continue south on 2nd Avenue East to reach Harrison Park and the Grey Roots Museum. Owen Sound has a walkable downtown core. You can get around town during the day on **Owen Sound Transit** buses (Downtown Transit Terminal, 1020 3rd Ave. E., 519/376-3299, www.owensound.ca, adults $2.50, students $2, under age 5 free), which operate 6:30am-6pm Monday-Friday and 9am-4pm Saturday. The useful Crosstown loop bus circles between downtown and Harrison Park.

To explore the surrounding towns or farther up the Bruce Peninsula, it's much easier to have your own wheels. It's about a 45-minute drive to Wiarton and 75-90 minutes to Tobermory. Several major car rental companies have offices in Owen Sound, including **Enterprise Rent-A-Car** (www.enterpriserentacar.ca), **Thrifty Car Rental** (www.thrifty.com), and **Discount Car Rentals** (www.discountcar.com).

Collingwood and the Blue Mountains

The Blue Mountain Resort, just outside the town of Collingwood, is Ontario's top ski destination. If you're expecting the Alps or the Rockies, you may chuckle when you see the size of the "mountains" here, but these rolling hills have enough terrain to keep most skiers or snowboarders occupied for at least several days. Besides the winter snow-sports season, the busiest times are midsummer (for mountain biking, hiking, golfing, and other outdoor activities) and fall weekends, when the trees blaze with color.

Collingwood (population 19,000) serves skiers and other outdoor adventurers with grocery stores, movie theaters, and excellent restaurants; it's a good base for exploring the region. If your goal is skiing, snowboarding, or other active pursuits, it's most convenient to stay in the Village at Blue Mountain, the resort area at the mountain base.

BLUE MOUNTAIN RESORT

Owned by resort giant Intrawest, **Blue Mountain Resort** (108 Jozo Weider Blvd., 705/445-0231 or 877/445-0231, www.blue-mountain.ca) is a car-free village, where casually upscale restaurants, bars, and outdoor clothing shops line the pedestrian streets. You can easily walk from village lodgings to the lifts; if you stay in one of the village condo developments, a free shuttle will pick you up.

Blue Mountain Activity Central (705/443-5522) acts as an activity concierge for guests. Staff keep a schedule of regular events, including free guided hikes or snowshoe tours, sleigh rides, scavenger hunts, toboggan tours, and more, plus activities for kids and teens. They also book activities both on and off the mountain. Prices for many mountain activities are discounted for guests staying in Blue Mountain Village lodgings.

Special events take place at Blue Mountain nearly every weekend from July through early

October and on select weekends during the rest of the year. Highlights include the **May Long Weekend Music and Fireworks** (late May), **Salsa at Blue Festival** (late June), **Village Beach Party** (early Aug.), and **Apple Harvest Festival** (early Oct.).

Skiing and Snowboarding

Blue Mountain Resort began life as a winter sports mecca and now has 15 lifts serving 42 trails. At 720 vertical feet, it's not a tall mountain, nor does it get buried in snow like western resorts, but an extensive snow-making operation supplements the average annual snowfall of 280 centimeters (110 inches). The winter season typically starts in December and runs through March. Come midweek to avoid the crowds.

Lift tickets (adults $64, seniors and ages 6-17 $44) are good for either day skiing (9am-4:30pm) or afternoon-night skiing (12:30pm-10pm). If you just want to ski in the evening (4:30pm-10pm), when 30 of the trails are open, tickets are adults $39, seniors and ages 6-17 $34. Ski and snowboard rentals, lessons, and kids camps are all available. For snowboarders, a **terrain park** (9am-9pm daily) has its own chairlift. To access the park, you must purchase a one-time $10 park pass in addition to your lift ticket.

Mountain Biking

From spring through fall, mountain bikers take over the trails at Blue Mountain Resort. The lifts are open to bikers 10am-8pm daily late June-early September, 10am-5pm Friday-Sunday late May-late June, and 10am-5pm Friday-Sunday early September-mid-October. Daily trail passes are $6 (no lift access), $15 (one lift access), or $38 (unlimited lift access). You can rent bikes and safety gear. A variety of guided mountain-biking options are available for youth, teens, adults, and families, both novice and experienced riders.

Collingwood and the Blue Mountains

© AVALON TRAVEL

Swimming and Water Sports

The year-round **Plunge Aquatic Centre** (200 Gord Canning Dr., 705/444-8705, www.plungebluemountain.ca, adults $15, ages 3-12 $12, families $42) adjacent to the Westin Trillium House, entertains water-lovers with indoor and outdoor swimming pools, several water slides, rope swings, hot tubs, and a water playground for toddlers. Schedules vary seasonally, but in general, Plunge is open daily in summer and winter, weekends only in spring and fall.

Admission tickets are good for a three-hour period.

In summer, Blue Mountain Resort maintains a **beach** (Blue Mountain Activity Central, 705/443-5522) on Georgian Bay, open only to resort guests. A complimentary 10-minute shuttle ride will take you from the village to the beach.

Mountain Coaster

Thrill-seekers should head for the **Ridge Runner Mountain Coaster** (daily

Wild Winter Adventures

Ontario may not have the towering mountains of western Canada, but that doesn't mean you can't take to the slopes. Not only do the Georgian Bay and Cottage Country regions north of Toronto have several spots for downhill skiing and snowboarding, but there are plenty of opportunities for cross-country skiing, snowshoeing, dogsledding, and other winter adventures. The Ottawa Valley region, a short drive from the nation's capital, is the other major Ontario destination for winter sports.

Blue Mountain Resort (705/445-0231 or 877/445-0231, www.bluemountain.ca) is the largest downhill ski resort in Ontario and offers mountain biking and other outdoor sports when the snow season ends. Closer to Toronto, **Horseshoe Resort** (1101 Horseshoe Valley Rd., Barrie, 705/835-2790 or 800/461-5627, www.horseshoeresort.com), north of Barrie off Highway 400, has downhill skiing and snowboarding, fat-tire snow biking, tubing, snowshoeing, and ice-skating in winter, plus golf, mountain biking, treetop trekking, among other summer activities.

For more places to ski or snowboard, check the **Ontario Snow Resorts Association** (www.skiontario.ca) or make tracks to these mountain resorts:

- **Calabogie Peaks Resort** (30 Barrett Chute Rd., Calabogie, 613/752-2720 or 800/669-4861, www.calabogie.com)

- **Dagmar Ski Resort** (1220 Lake Ridge Rd., Uxbridge, 905/649-2002, www.skidagmar.com)

- **Hidden Valley Highlands Ski Area** (1655 Hidden Valley Rd., Huntsville, 705/789-1773 or 800/398-9555, www.skihiddenvalley.on.ca)

- **Hockley Valley Resort** (793522 3rd Line EHS, Mono, 519/942-0754 or 866/462-5539, www.hockley.com)

- **Lakeridge** (790 Chalk Lake Rd., Uxbridge, 905/649-2058, www.ski-lakeridge.com)

- **Mount Pakenham** (577 Ski Hill Rd., Pakenham, 613/624-5290, www.mountpakenham.com)

- **Mount St. Louis Moonstone** (24 Mount St. Louis Rd., Coldwater, 705/835-2112, www.mountstlouis.com)

- **Searchmont Ski Resort** (103 Searchmont Resort Rd., Searchmont, 705/781-2340, www.searchmont.com)

mid-May-Oct., Sat.-Sun. mid-Dec.-Mar., over age 12 $15 per ride, ages 3-12 $6 per ride), which twists and turns from the top of the Glades area through the trees and down to the village. One or two people can ride together in each car, and riders control the car's speed. For specific operating hours, which vary seasonally, check with Blue Mountain Activity Central (705/443-5522, www.bluemountain.ca).

Summer Activities

Two different ropes courses test your agility and balance. On the family-friendly **Woodlot Low Ropes** (daily mid-May-Oct., over age 12 $25, ages 6-12 $20), navigate three routes at different heights, crossing beams, ropes, suspended logs, and other swaying aerial elements. The tougher **Timber Challenge High Ropes** (daily mid-May-Oct., over age 12 $59) comprises seven different courses that take you more than 15 meters (50 feet) above the forest floor.

Another activity for the adventurous, the **Wind Rider Triple Zips** (daily mid-May-Oct., over age 12 $15, ages 10-12 $12) includes two 122-meter (400-foot) zip lines. Three lines run in parallel, letting you zip with friends or family members. On the **Apex Bagjump** (daily mid-May-Oct., over age 12 $15, ages 8-12 $12), you free-fall from four increasingly higher platforms into a puffy airbag on the ground.

Still want more things to do? Hiking, tennis, golf, miniature golf, indoor rock climbing, mountaintop Segway tours, and riding the **Blue Mountain Gondola** (late May-mid-Oct., over age 12 $15, under age 12 $12) are among the many other mountain activities.

Accommodations

Blue Mountain Village has several hotel and condominium properties, and just outside the village are additional condo and townhouse complexes. You can book lodgings through **Blue Mountain Central Reservations** (877/445-0231, www.bluemountain.ca). When booking, ask whether the lodging is ski-in, ski-out or within walking distance of the lifts. Winter room rates typically start at about $150 d, and a variety of lodging and lift ticket packages are available.

The **Blue Mountain Inn** was the village's original lodging, and while it's starting to show its age, it offers moderately priced accommodations. You can walk to the Century Express chair lift. For more style, the boutique **Mosaïc** has 163 contemporary suites, ranging from studios to three-bedroom units. The smaller units have kitchenettes, and the larger suites, some of which are multilevel townhouses, have full kitchens. There's a fitness center as well as a year-round outdoor pool and hot tub. It's not as close to the lifts as the **Weider Lodge** or the **Grand Georgian**—both slightly older, well-appointed condo hotels—but the rooms are more stylish and you can walk to the gondola in a few minutes.

The village's most upscale lodging, a short walk from the gondola, is the **Westin Trillium House** (220 Gord Canning Dr., 705/443-8080 or 800/937-8461, www.westinbluemountain.com, $195-550 d), designed like a grand Georgian Bay lodge. The 222 spacious units, including standard guest rooms and one-, two-, and three-bedroom suites, have modern furnishings in ski-lodge beiges and browns, as well as TV/DVDs and kitchenettes. There's a 24-hour gym, year-round outdoor pool, sauna, and hot tubs. If you're too tired to walk downstairs to the restaurant or lounge, you can order from room service.

Food

Food in the village tends toward either fare to fuel up fast and get back on the slopes or simple but hearty pub-style eats. For more dining options, head to the nearby towns of Thornbury to the west or Collingwood to the east. Start your day with coffee and pastry at the **Royal Majesty Espresso Bar Bakery**

Georgian Bay views from the Blue Mountain Gondola

(190 Jozo Weider Blvd., 705/812-3476, www. royalmajesty.ca, generally 7am-9pm daily), or stop in later for soup or a sandwich. Free Wi-Fi.

The local outpost of a Toronto-based restaurant group, **Oliver and Bonacini Café Grill** (Westin Trillium House, 220 Gord Canning Dr., 705/444-8680, www.oliver-bonacini.com, 7am-10pm daily, lunch $13-27, dinner $15-42) is one of the best places to eat in the village. The contemporary dishes—chopped salad with romaine, arugula, pickled squash, and pumpkin seeds; shrimp linguine with almond pesto; pork chops with spice-roasted sweet potatoes and apple chutney—are both crowd-pleasing and creative.

It's worth the 20-minute drive to ★ **Bruce Wine Bar and Kitchen** (8 Bruce St., Thornbury, 519/599-1112, www.brucewinebar.ca, 11:30am-close Tues.-Sun., $15-28), which emphasizes local ingredients in its imaginative sharing plates, wood-fired pizzas, and entrées. The pies range from traditional to unusual; try the excellent version topped with smoked trout, pea sprouts, cherry tomatoes, and pickled onions. While the entrées change regularly, they always include a "daily beast" (perhaps duck, rabbit, or venison) and sustainable seafood. The wine list highlights Canadian labels and by-the-glass options; the vibe at the rustic wood tables or along the bar is welcoming and informal.

Information and Services

Blue Mountain Resort is 170 kilometers (105 miles) northwest of Toronto and 11 kilometers (7 miles) west of Collingwood, off Highway 26. Depending on traffic and weather conditions, it's about a two-hour drive from metropolitan Toronto. For resort information or reservations, contact **Blue Mountain Resorts** (108 Jozo Weider Blvd., 705/445-0231 or 877/445-0231, www.bluemountain.ca); you can also get information from the **Blue Mountain Village Association** (705/444-7398, www.bluemountainvillage.ca).

Getting Around

If you're staying in the Village at Blue Mountain, you don't need a car. The village is car-free (and ringed with parking lots where you can leave yours). A free **resort shuttle** (www.bluemountain.ca) loops through the village daily every 15-20 minutes between 8am and 10:30pm. Outside of these hours, call for a pickup by dialing extension 8280 on any resort phone.

COLLINGWOOD

While many people come to Collingwood to ski or snowboard at nearby Blue Mountain, it's also a pleasant spot for a weekend getaway, even if you're not mountain-bound. The Collingwood area draws gourmets to its many first-rate restaurants. The **Georgian Trail** (www.georgiantrail.ca) is a flat, 34-kilometer (21-mile) rail trail for hiking and cycling that runs west from Collingwood to the towns of Thornbury and Meaford, passing several beaches en route. In winter, it's a cross-country ski and snowshoeing trail.

To soothe those post-adventure sore muscles, sink into the outdoor baths at the **Scandinave Spa at Blue Mountain** (152 Grey Road 21, Blue Mountains, 705/443-8484 or 877/988-8484, www.scandinave.com, 10am-9pm daily, $50, Wed. $40), which offers a Scandinavian-style "bath experience." First, warm up in one of the Finnish saunas, steam baths, or outdoor hot tubs. Then immerse yourself in a chilling plunge pool. After recovering in a relaxation area, repeat the process until you feel totally tranquil; the average stay is 2-4 hours. The experience is even more magical when snow falls on the hot pools. Bathing suits are required, and you must be at least 19 years old.

For several days in July, Collingwood is overrun with Elvis Presley lookalikes. The annual **Collingwood Elvis Festival** (866/444-1162, www.collingwoodelvisfestival.com) features a parade and more than 100 tribute concerts; it ranks among the world's largest Elvis festivals.

Scenic Caves Nature Adventures

Located in the hills outside Collingwood, **Scenic Caves Nature Adventures** (260-280 Scenic Caves Rd., 705/446-0256, www.sceniccaves.com, 9am-8pm daily late-June-early Sept., call or check the website for spring and fall hours, adults $23, seniors $21, ages 3-17 $19) is a sprawling outdoor playground. Walking trails wind through the woods, and you can explore a network of underground **caves** (try to squeeze through "Fat Man's Misery," a narrow rock channel). A highlight is a stroll across the 126-meter (413-foot) **suspension bridge**, one of Ontario's longest suspension footbridges, with panoramic views across Georgian Bay. Admission rates include access to the caves, suspension bridge, and walking trails.

At 777-meters (2,550-feet) long, the **Thunderbird Twin Zip Line** (adults $48, seniors $46, ages 10-17 $44) is Canada's longest twin zip line, with two zip lines side-by-side and vistas across the Blue Mountains and Georgian Bay. Tickets for the Twin Zip Line include access to the caves, suspension bridge, and trails.

Another option is a three-hour guided ecotour (adults $95, seniors and ages 10-17 $85), which includes a short hike to the suspension bridge, followed by a treetop canopy tour through the trees on a network of narrow wooden bridges. You'll also tour the caves and whiz through the air on two zip lines, including a 305-meter (1,000-foot) plunge from the top of the Niagara Escarpment.

In winter, the park is open for cross-country skiing and snowshoeing (9am-5pm daily Dec.-Mar., full-day pass: adults $19 weekend, $15 weekday, seniors and ages 6-17 $15 weekend, $13 weekday). You can even snowshoe across the suspension bridge. Ski and snowshoe rentals are available.

Allow a minimum of two hours to explore the site, but you can easily spend most of the day. Wear running or hiking shoes. There's a small snack bar, but for more variety, pack your own picnic lunch.

Accommodations

A number of Collingwood's restored Victorian homes are now inns or B&Bs, and in the hills around town, you'll find more small accommodations. Contact the **Collingwood Area Bed-and-Breakfast Association** (www.bbcanada.com) for additional lodging options. Motels are clustered west of town along Highway 26.

crossing the suspension bridge at Scenic Caves Nature Adventures

The **Beild House Country Inn** (64 3rd St., 705/444-1522 or 888/322-3453, www.beildhouse.com, $140-150 d) is just a block from Collingwood's main downtown street, but it has the faded charm of a country estate. The parlor, with its dark woodwork and chintz sofas, and the dining room, where elaborate multicourse dinners are served by candlelight, recall its glory days as a private residence. The 11 guest rooms are romantic in a cozy, if slightly fussy, Victorian style. Rates include full breakfast and afternoon tea. If you're not staying at the inn, you can have dinner ($55-65) with advance reservations.

The four guest rooms at romantic **Bacchus House** (142 Hume St., 705/446-4700, www.bacchushouse.ca, call for rates) are decorated with a wine theme: the purple Pinot Noir Suite has an ornate four-poster bed, and the Cabernet Sauvignon Suite has a claw-foot tub. Common spaces in this 1880 yellow-brick Victorian include the living room, with a fireplace, a deck with a hot tub, and the dining room where a full breakfast is served. Only the location on a busy street mars the elegance of this upscale lodging; the golden-hued Chardonnay Suite at the rear of the house is the quietest.

Set on a six-hectare (15-acre) property with gardens, walking trails, a swimming pool, and a gaggle of ducks and hens, the **Willow Trace B&B** (7833 Poplar Side Rd., 705/445-9003, www.collingwoodbedandbreakfast.com, $130-155 d) feels like a rural getaway, yet it's only a five-minute drive from downtown. The rooms are bright and modern, with two upstairs and one that's family-friendly on the lower level facing the gardens. Among the breakfast options that co-owner and chef Philip Tarlo, who runs the B&B with his wife, Leanne Calvert, prepares are cinnamon french toast, customized omelets, or a full English breakfast.

Food

Collingwood's restaurants range from the foodie to the ardently epicurean. Most are located on or near Hurontario Street in the town center.

Hidden in a lane downtown, **Tesoro** (18 School House Lane, 705/444-9230, www.tesororestaurant.ca, 11am-11pm Mon.-Sat. fall-spring, 11am-10pm Mon.-Sat. winter., lunch $9-20, dinner $15-35), with its sturdy pine tables and vibrant red chairs, is the sort of welcoming, casual Italian eatery everyone would like to have in their neighborhood. There's a long list of creative pizzas (try the Tre Funghi, with black olives and three types of mushrooms), as well as updated versions of Italian classics like penne *arrabbiata* (pasta with spicy sausage and hot peppers), chicken parmigiano, or lasagna.

In an 1889 former hotel, the classy **Tremont Café** (80 Simcoe St., 705/293-6000, www.thetremontcafe.com, 10am-11pm Wed.-Mon., lunch $11-16, dinner $16-36), with a curved bar, white-painted woodwork, and floor-to-ceiling windows, invites lingering, with daytime coffee, evening drinks, and lunch (11am-3pm) and dinner (5:30pm-9:30pm) in between. On the plate, expect well-crafted dishes with lots of seasonal ingredients: a lemon-tahini-dressed veggie bowl, hearty salads, or shrimp tacos mid-day, and heartier fare, from short ribs with harissa and wilted greens to duck confit paired with parsnip purée, for supper.

One of Ontario's most distinctive dining destinations is ★ **Eigensinn Farm** (449357 Concession Rd. 10, Singhampton, 519/922-3128, www.stadtlanderseigensinnfarm.com), which draws well-heeled gourmets from far and wide. Chef-owner Michael Stadtlander, with his wife and business partner, Nobuyo, accommodate no more than a dozen diners nightly, creating extravagant eight-course tasting menus ($275-300). And that's not including wine; the restaurant has no liquor license, so guests bring their own. The restaurant's schedule can be as wildly personal as the dining experience, so make reservations well in advance. It's about 13 kilometers (eight miles) south Collingwood via County Road 124.

The owners of Eigensinn Farm run the nearby **Haisai Restaurant & Bakery** (794079 County Rd. 124, Singhampton, 705/445-2748, www.haisairestaurantbakery.com, no credit cards). The bakery (11am-4pm Fri.-Sun.) sells freshly baked breads and pastries, along with a selection of prepared foods. The restaurant (11am-3pm Fri.-Sun.) serves imaginative pizzas, dim sum, and other dishes with locally sourced ingredients.

Information and Services

The **Georgian Triangle Tourist Association** (45 St. Paul St., 705/445-7722 or 888/227-8667, www.visitsouthgeorgianbay.ca) runs a visitor information center that provides information about the Collingwood-Blue Mountain region. **Greyhound Bus Lines** (800/661-8747, www.greyhound.ca) operates one daily bus in each direction between Toronto and Collingwood (3 hours); the same buses also go on to Blue Mountain. In town, the buses depart from Collingwood's **Transportation Centre** (22 2nd St., 705/445-7095). On the mountain, buses stop at the **Blue Mountain Inn** (www.bluemountain.ca).

Getting There and Around

Simcoe County Airport Service (705/728-1148 or 800/461-7529, www.simcoecountyairportservice.ca) runs regular vans from Toronto's Pearson Airport to Collingwood and the Blue Mountain Resort. Prices vary depending on the number of people in your party. From Pearson Airport to Collingwood, the one-way price is $97 for one person, $130 for two; to Blue Mountain, it's $109 for one, $143 for two. **Colltrans** (705/446-1196, www.collingwood.ca, 6:30am-9pm Mon.-Fri., 7am-6pm Sat., 9am-5pm Sun., $2) is the town's public transportation service, with several routes around the community and between Collingwood and Blue Mountain.

VICINITY OF COLLINGWOOD

Several small towns around Collingwood, including Thornbury and Meaford to the west and Creemore to the south, are worth exploring for their galleries, shops, and restaurants. Wasaga Beach, the world's longest freshwater beach, is also an easy day trip from Collingwood.

Creemore

This village of about 1,300 people makes a great day trip if you're looking for that elusive "small-town charm." The main downtown street—Mill Street—is lined with art galleries, cafés, and shops, ready-made for wandering and browsing. Creemore's main attraction is the **Creemore Springs Brewery** (139 Mill St., 705/466-2240 or 800/267-2240, www.creemoresprings.com, 10am-6pm Mon.-Sat., 11am-5pm Sun.), started in 1987 by three beer-loving guys who retired to the area and decided they needed a hobby. The brewery produces several varieties of beer, including their signature Creemore Springs Premium Lager. Free 30-minute tours, offered several times a day year-round, wrap up with a beer tasting.

The **Mad and Noisy Gallery** (154 Mill St., 705/466-5555, www.madandnoisy.com, 11am-5pm Mon.-Fri., 10am-5pm Sat., noon-4pm Sun. summer, call for off-season hours) is neither—it's named for the two rivers that meet near Creemore. It showcases high-quality work of painters, sculptors, photographers, and other artists, most of whom hail from the Southern Georgian Bay area. The **Maplestone Gallery** (142 Mill St., 705/520-0067, www.maplestonegallery.com, 11am-5pm Thurs.-Fri., 10am-5pm Sat., 11am-4pm Sun.) is unique in Canada for displaying only contemporary mosaic art. Many of the works are surprisingly ornate and, not surprisingly, beautiful. Want to learn to create mosaics yourself? The gallery runs periodic workshops for beginners.

Mill Street has several cafés, bakeries, and restaurants, as well as the **100 Mile Store** (176 Mill St., 705/466-3514, www.100milestore.ca), a local grocery that sources its products—from produce and meats to snacks, cheeses, and ice cream—within 100 miles of town.

The sign outside **Creemore Kitchen** (134 Mill St., 705/466-2900, www.creemorekitchen. ca, lunch 11am-2:30pm, dinner from 5:30pm Wed.-Mon., $8.50-28) says, "Seasonal. Local. Good Food," and that's what you get at this modern country kitchen in a cute country house. At lunch, try one of the sandwiches, like the Asian-inspired pork belly with pickled carrots on a steamed bun, and in the evening, your options might include Filipino-style spring rolls with onion-tomato jam, a seasonally changing pasta, or fried chicken with biscuits and gravy. There's a **bakery** (11am-4pm) if you'd like something sweet.

When you're done shopping and snacking, venture east of Mill Street to find the **Creemore Jail** (Library St., between Elizabeth St. and Caroline St.). This diminutive stone structure, built in 1892, claims to be the smallest jail in North America.

Creemore is about 30 kilometers (19 miles) southeast of Collingwood. Take Highway 26 east from Collingwood to Highway 42 south; then go west on Highway 9 into Creemore and turn left onto Mill Street.

Wasaga Beach

The Wasaga area had a part in the War of 1812, through a trading ship called the *Nancy.* Built in 1789, the *Nancy* was pressed into service as a British supply vessel. In 1814, American troops attacked the *Nancy* on the Nottawasaga River. The ship sank, and over the next century, the silt and sand flowing through the river collected around the ship's hull, preserving the remains and forming an island around the boat.

The *Nancy* was excavated in the 1920s, and today, at the **Nancy Island Historic Site** (119 Mosley St., 705/429-2728, www.wasagabeachpark.com, 10am-6pm daily mid-June-early Sept., 10am-6pm Sat.-Sun. late May-mid-June and early Sept.-mid-Oct.), you can see the *Nancy*'s hull, watch a video about her story, and join in as park staff reenact elements of the *Nancy*'s history. Also on the site is the **Wasaga Beach Welcome Centre**, which has information about the *Nancy* and

the surrounding area, a small museum, and a replica of an 1884 lighthouse that once stood near Collingwood's harbor.

Along Georgian Bay, **Wasaga Beach Provincial Park** (11 22nd St. N., 705/429-2516, www.ontarioparks.com, 8:15am-10pm daily Apr.-mid-Oct., Apr.-late June and early Sept.-mid-Oct. $20 per vehicle, late June-early Sept. $16-20) is the world's longest freshwater beach. This stretch of sand extends for 14 kilometers (nearly nine miles) and is divided into eight different sections, each with a different personality. Beaches 1 to 4 are closer into town and have more restaurants, shops, and other services; they're also more crowded and honky-tonk. As you move farther from the town center—to beaches 5 and 6 to the south and New Wasaga and Allenwood Beaches to the north—the sand becomes less populated and more peaceful. Because the beach is flat and the bay is shallow, Wasaga is a popular destination for families.

Although most people come for the beach, Wasaga also has 50 kilometers (31 miles) of hiking trails. The park service leads guided hikes on selected Wednesdays in July and August. In winter, there are 30 kilometers (19 miles) of trails for cross-country skiing. Access the trail network from the **Wasaga Nordic Centre** (101 Blueberry Trail, 705/429-0943, 9am-5pm daily mid-Dec.-mid-Mar., adults $13, ages 6-17 $6).

The **Town of Wasaga Beach** (705/429-3844, www.wasagabeach.com) and the **Wasaga Beach Chamber of Commerce** (705/429-2247 or 866/292-7242, www.wasagainfo.com) are good sources of information about accommodations and services in the Wasaga area, which includes the usual assortment of modest beach motels, plus privately run campgrounds (the provincial park has no camping facilities). The Chamber can provide details about cottage rentals. Located about 20 kilometers (12.5 miles) east of Collingwood, Wasaga Beach is an easy day trip; take Highway 26 to Highway 92.

Midland and Parry Sound

The peninsula on Georgian Bay's southwestern side that houses the towns of Midland and Penetanguishene played an important role in Ontario's early history. Long populated by First Nations people, in the 1600s a site near present-day Midland became the region's first European settlement, when a group of French Jesuits established a village. Several interesting historic sites, particularly the well-designed Sainte-Marie Among the Hurons, illuminate the region's past. The area retains a strong French and First Nations heritage.

Like other areas around Georgian Bay, the Midland region has its share of beautiful outdoor destinations, particularly Wye Marsh in Midland and the large Awenda Provincial Park in Penetanguishene. It's also a gateway to the 30,000 Islands region of Georgian Bay, some of which are protected in Georgian Bay Islands National Park. You can visit Georgian Bay Islands National Park in a day trip from Midland or Penetanguishene; it's less than an hour's drive to Honey Harbour, where the boat to the park islands departs.

North along Georgian Bay is Parry Sound, a pleasant community that's both a cultural destination and a base for outdoor activities; the ruggedly beautiful Killbear Provincial Park nearby draws travelers to its shores and waterfront campgrounds.

MIDLAND

The largest community along this part of Georgian Bay, Midland (population 17,000) still retains a low-key small-town feel along King Street, the main downtown street. The town has begun to sprawl out from the center, with malls and other developments, and its sights are spread around the area, but it's a convenient base for exploring the region's historic and outdoor attractions.

As you walk around downtown Midland, look for the 34 wall **murals** (www.

downtownmidland.ca). One mural, painted on silos along Midland Harbor, depicts a Jesuit priest and a Wendat indigenous person at Sainte-Marie; it is reportedly the largest outdoor historic mural in North America. Pick up a mural map at the harbor-front **Midland Visitor Information Centre** (165 King St., 705/527-4050 or 855/527-4050, www.midland.ca, 9am-8pm daily May-Sept.).

★ Sainte-Marie Among the Hurons

In 1639, a group of French Jesuit missionaries began constructing a community near present-day Midland, establishing the first European settlement in Ontario. Their goal was to bring Christianity to the indigenous Wendat people, whom they called the "Hurons." The Jesuits worked with the Wendat for 10 years, until hostilities worsened between the Wendat and the nearby Iroquois people. After two priests were killed in skirmishes with the Iroquois, the Jesuits abandoned the settlement and burned it to the ground to protect it from desecration. Centuries later, in 1930, Pope Pius XI canonized the murdered priests, Jean de Brébeuf and Gabriel Lalemant.

What you see today at the fascinating historic village **Sainte-Marie Among the Hurons** (Hwy. 12 E., 705/526-7838, www.saintemarieamongthehurons.on.ca, 10am-5pm daily mid-May-mid-Oct., 10am-5pm Mon.-Fri. late Apr.-mid-May and late Oct., adults $12, seniors $10, students $10.50, ages 6-12 $9.25) is a "reimagination" of the 17th-century settlement. Because the Jesuits left no records, historians can only theorize what the community actually looked like. It wasn't until the 1940s and 1950s that archeologists began excavating the area, providing clues to the village's history and structure.

Sainte-Marie was reconstructed replicating French construction styles of the period.

Midland and Penetanguishene

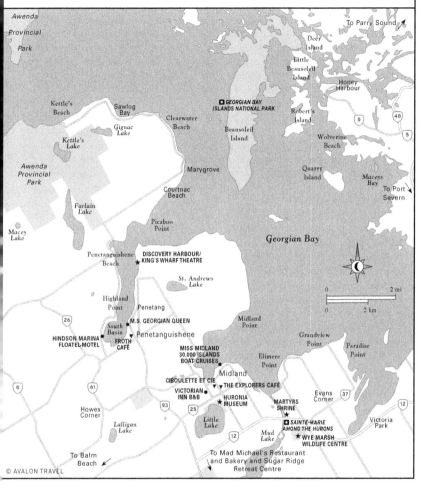

Surrounded by a high wooden fence, the settlement has 25 buildings in three main areas. The **North Court** was the mission's primary living and working quarters, including a cookhouse, chapel, carpentry shop, a chicken run, and stables. The **South Court,** where supplies arrived following an 800-mile canoe journey from Quebec, has a reconstructed waterway with working locks. The third section of the settlement was the **Native Area,** where a church, a longhouse, a hospital, and other structures illustrate the mix of French and Wendat building styles and cultures.

You can easily spend several hours exploring the settlement. Start your visit with the 15-minute movie that introduces the site's history. In summer, costumed guides staff the village buildings, demonstrating elements of village life, from cooking to blacksmithing to Wendat storytelling. In spring or fall, when fewer staff are on duty, pick up the audio guide ($3 summer, free spring and fall) to help understand the site. Following your walk through the village, you can explore museum exhibits that provide more background and history about the settlement.

Sainte-Marie Among the Hurons organizes special events throughout the year. Highlights include the annual **Aboriginal Festival** (June), which honors the Wendat heritage with traditional dancing, music, games, and crafts, and the **First Light Festival** (late Nov.), which lights up the Sainte-Marie site with more than 3,000 candles.

The site is five kilometers (three miles) east on Highway 12 from the intersection of Highway 93.

Wye Marsh Wildlife Centre

A lovely spot to enjoy the outdoors is the nature center and marshlands at **Wye Marsh Wildlife Centre** (16160 Hwy. 12 E., 705/526-7809, www.wyemarsh.com, 9am-5pm daily, adults $11, seniors and students $8.50, ages 4-12 $8, families $30) on Midland's east side, next to Sainte-Marie Among the Hurons. The visitors center has exhibits about local ecology, and kids enjoy the live animal presentations, but the real action is outdoors on the network of walking trails. Rent an audio guide about the plants and wildlife, or simply follow the interpretive signs; climb the observation tower for views over the marsh.

The marsh is a nesting habitat for **trumpeter swans,** and one highlight of a visit here is the chance to observe these majestic birds. You can canoe or kayak on the channels that wind through the marsh, and guided canoe excursions ($8 pp) are offered. In winter, there are 22 kilometers (14 miles) of groomed trails for cross-country skiing and 10 kilometers (six miles) of snowshoeing trails. Ski ($15) and snowshoe rentals ($5-10) are available. A variety of other nature programs are offered throughout the year.

Martyrs' Shrine

Across the highway from Sainte-Marie Among the Hurons, the 1926 **Martyrs' Shrine** (16163 Hwy. 12 W., 705/526-3788, www.martyrs-shrine.com, 8am-9pm daily mid-May-mid-Oct., over age 11 $5, up to $20 per vehicle), with its two soaring spires, honors the memory of the two Jesuits who worked at Sainte-Marie but died in a 1649 Iroquois raid. Roman Catholic mass is held several times a day, and you can stroll the gardens and walkways. The site draws religious pilgrims from all over the world.

Huronia Museum

Exploring the **Huronia Museum** (549 Little Lake Park, 705-526-2844, www.huronia-museum.com, 9am-5pm daily May-Oct., 9am-5pm Mon.-Fri. Nov.-Apr., adults $10, seniors $7, ages 5-17 $5), an old-fashioned regional history museum, feels like a treasure hunt. You might find everything from washtubs to wheelchairs, sewing machines to the Slenderizer (an old-time exercise machine). Most of the hodgepodge of artifacts dates from the 1800s and 1900s. Also on the site is the Huron Ouendat Village, a modest re-creation of a 16th-century First Nations settlement.

Sports and Recreation

The Midland-Penetanguishene peninsula is surrounded by water, but many of the beaches are private. One exception is the small, sandy **Balm Beach** (www.visitbalmbeach.com) on Georgian Bay, a pretty spot to watch the sunset. From Midland, take Highway 25/Balm Beach Road directly west to the water. The **Miss Midland 30,000 Islands Boat Cruises** (705/549-3388, www.midlandtours.com, mid-May-mid-Oct., adults $28, seniors $26, students $21, ages 5-14 $15) are two-hour tours around Georgian Bay Islands National Park and some of the other islands in the 30,000 Islands region. Cruises depart from the Midland Town Dock at the foot of King Street.

Accommodations

Midland has the usual selection of chain motels, clustered along King Street near Highway 12 or on Yonge Street off Highway 93. Try the **Best Western Highland Inn** (924 King

St., 705/526-9307 or 800/461-4265, www. bestwesternmidland.com) or the **Midland Comfort Inn** (980 King St., 705/526-2090 or 888/274-3020, www.comfortinn.com). For more bed-and-breakfast options, check the website of the **Southern Georgian Bay B&B Association** (www.southerngeorgian-baybb.com).

You feel like part of the family when you stay at **The Victorian Inn Bed & Breakfast** (670 Hugel Ave., 705/526-4441 or 877/450-7660, www.victorianinn.ca, $119-149), a bright-yellow house with a wraparound porch. Two of the three homey guest rooms, with quilt-topped beds, have en suite baths; the larger Royal Suite has a separate sitting area and a private bath across the hall. Well-traveled owners Peter and Kim Hakkenberg have filled the dining room, where they serve a full breakfast, with mementos of their journeys. Children under age 12 are not permitted.

Set amid marshlands south of Midland, the peaceful ★ **Sugar Ridge Retreat Centre** (5720 Forgets Rd., Wyebridge, 705/528-1793 or 866/609-1793, www.sugarridge.ca, $149 s or d, includes breakfast) offers yoga retreats and other workshops. Owners Liz and Kurt Frost have 10 sturdy, simply furnished cabins, which sleep up to four, in the fields around the main lodge, a contemporary Zen-style retreat center with an airy yoga studio and large dining room. Cabins have no plumbing, phones, or Internet; restrooms, showers, and Wi-Fi are available in the lodge, where breakfast is served. Guests are welcome to join in **yoga classes** (nonguests $15).

Food

For places to eat in Midland, wander along King Street downtown. At **Ciboulette et Cie** (248 King St., 705/245-0410, www.cibouletteetcie.ca, 8am-6am Mon.-Thurs. and Sat., 8am-7pm Fri., 10am-4pm Sun.), a cheerful café and takeout shop (the name is French for "Chives and Co."), the day starts with freshly baked scones and other pastries. Creative sandwiches and delicious ready-to-eat salads, perhaps Brussels sprout slaw or roasted sweet potatoes with cranberries, make a quick lunch.

With its walls of books, maps, and photos of faraway lands, **The Explorers Cafe** (345 King St., 705/527-9199, www.theexplorerscafe.com, noon-10pm Tues.-Sat., lunch $10-17, dinner $21-32) resembles a Victorian-era adventurer's residence. The menu wanders the world, too, from Indian curry to Argentinean steak to East African-style shrimp. Despite the international emphasis, there's usually a "100-mile meal," with most ingredients locally sourced. Although the restaurant is right downtown, you may need a compass to find it, since it's set back from the main road; look for their signboard on King Street.

Craving Texas-style barbecue pork ribs? Jerk chicken? Barbecue brisket? Head for the little yellow bungalow, about 10 minutes south of Midland, that houses **MAD Michael's Restaurant and Bakery** (8215 Hwy. 93, Wyebridge, 705/527-1666, www.madmichaels.com, noon-8pm Thurs.-Sun. May-mid-Oct., lunch $9-20, dinner $15-25). This isn't any ordinary barbecue shack; chef "Mad" Michael White smokes ribs in his outdoor kitchen, bakes bread, and in his spare time, crafts rustic wood furniture. Save room for a slice of homemade pie.

Practicalities

The **Midland Visitor Information Centre** (165 King St., 705/527-4050 or 855/527-4050, www.midland.ca, 9am-8pm daily May-Sept.), near the waterfront downtown, has lots of information about the region. The Midland-Penetanguishene area is about 160 kilometers (100 miles) from Toronto. From Highway 93, take Highway 12 east, then turn left onto King Street for downtown Midland or continue east on Highway 12 to Sainte-Marie Among the Hurons, the Martyrs' Shrine, and Wye Marsh. You need a car to explore the attractions around the region.

PENETANGUISHENE

Smaller than nearby Midland, the town of Penetanguishene (population 9,300) has a strong French heritage; roughly 16 percent of the residents speak French as their first language. Penetanguishene's main attractions are the restored naval base at Discovery Harbour and the sprawling Awenda Provincial Park, which has the region's best beaches. Penetanguishene Harbor is also the departure point for the area's most interesting 30,000 Islands cruise.

Discovery Harbour

Ahoy, matey! Climb aboard the replicas of two majestic 18th-century British sailing vessels, the HMS *Bee,* a supply schooner, and the HMS *Tecumseth,* a warship, at **Discovery Harbour** (93 Jury Dr., 705/549-8064, www. discoveryharbour.on.ca, 10am-5pm daily July-early Sept., 10am-5pm Mon.-Fri. late May-June, adults $7, seniors and students $6.25, ages 6-12 $5.25), a restored naval base that the British built following the War of 1812 to protect the Upper Great Lakes region from future American attacks. While only one original building remains (the 1845 Officers' Quarters), the reconstructed site reflects naval and military life here in the 1800s. Guides in period costumes conduct tours of the 19 historic buildings and demonstrate various aspects of sailors' lives, including cooking, rope

work, and games. Also on-site is the HMS. *Tecumseth* Centre, which houses the original hull of this 1815 warship, as well as exhibits about and artifacts from Penetanguishene during the War of 1812.

30,000 Island Cruises

What makes the island cruises special on the **MS *Georgian Queen*** (705/549-7795 or 800/363-7447, www.georgianbaycruises. com, May-mid-Oct., adults $20-27, seniors $18-24, ages 5-14 $9-11, families $49-65) is the onboard commentary that the companionable captain provides. As you cruise out of Penetanguishene Harbor and out among the 30,000 Islands, Captain Steve will not only point out the sights, but he'll tell you who lives on what island (many are private), which properties are for sale and at what price, and how locals manage to build homes, transport goods, and spend summers on these isolated chunks of rock. The 1.5- to 3.5-hour cruises depart from the Town Docks at the foot of Main Street. Take one of the longer cruises if you can, since the shortest excursions stay around the harbor.

Awenda Provincial Park

Fronting Georgian Bay 11 kilometers (seven

tall ships at Discovery Harbour

miles) northwest of Penetanguishene, the 2,915-hectare (7,200-acre) **Awenda Provincial Park** (Awenda Park Rd., off Concession Rd. 16 E./Lafontaine Rd. E., 705/549-2231, www.ontarioparks.com, $14.50 per vehicle) is a beautiful destination for hiking and swimming. One of central Ontario's largest parks, Awenda is in a transition zone between north and south, making it home to a diverse array of plants and trees, as well as roughly 200 bird species and many reptiles and amphibians. In summer, park staff offer nature programs, theatrical productions, and other special events; call the park office or check online with **Friends of Awenda** (www.awendapark.ca) for schedules.

The park has approximately 30 kilometers (19 miles) of multiuse trails. The most popular is the easy **Beach Trail,** which connects the park's four beaches. Off the Beach Trail, you can follow the easy, one-kilometer (0.6-mile) **Beaver Pond Trail,** most of which is along a boardwalk, to an area that had extensive beaver activity. Longer park trails include the **Robitaille Homestead Trail,** a three-kilometer (1.9-mile) round-trip trail past ancient sand dunes that begins in the day parking lot near Bear Campground; the five-kilometer (three-mile) **Wendat Trail,** which starts near Kettle's Lake; and the 13-kilometer (eight-mile) **Bluff Trail,** which circles the campgrounds and connects the camping areas to the beach.

Some of the area's nicest swimming spots are within the provincial park, which has four beaches along Georgian Bay. **First Beach,** closest to the parking area, is a sheltered, family-friendly sand beach that also has rocks for the kids to climb. You can continue along the beach trail to **Second Beach; Third Beach,** which has particularly soft sand; and eventually to the more secluded **Fourth Beach.** It's about two kilometers (1.25 miles) from First to Fourth Beach.

You can also swim at **Kettle's Lake,** an inland lake with an easy boardwalk trail to the water. The lake is a calm spot for canoeing,

particularly for beginning paddlers; in summer, canoe rentals are available. Around the lake, you might see otters, beavers, loons, or great blue herons. Awenda is open year-round, and you can cross-country ski here in winter.

Entertainment

Located at Discovery Harbour, the **King's Wharf Theatre** (97 Jury Dr., 705/549-5555, www.draytonentertainment.com) is a professional summer theater that produces several plays every year from June to early September.

Accommodations and Food

Catering primarily to boaters and their guests, the **Hindson Marina Floatel-Motel** (79 Champlain Rd., 705/549-2991, www.hindsonmarina.com, $125-179 d) is a floating lodging, right on the docks on the west side of Penetanguishene Harbor. The three rooms and one two-room suite are ordinary motel units, but you can't get much closer to the water than this. Entrance is through the marina gates.

Awenda Provincial Park's **Stone Cottage** (Awenda Park Rd., off Concession Rd. 16 E., 888/668-7275, www.ontarioparks.com, May-Oct., reservation fee online $11, by phone $13, late June-early Sept. $1,040 per week, May-June and Sept.-Oct. $150 per night) has a spacious terrace above the water and a huge living room with a stone fireplace and windows facing the bay. One bedroom has a double bed and two bunks, the other twin beds. It has no running water; drinking water is provided, and there's an outhouse but no shower. Bring sleeping bags or linens, food, and cooking gear. Make reservations well in advance.

Up the hill from Penetanguishene harbor, **Froth Café** (102 Main St., 705/549-7199, www.frothcafe.com, 8am-6pm Tues.-Sat., 9am-4pm Sun.) is convenient for breakfast, lunch, or a sightseeing coffee break. The menu is simple: scones, bagels, french toast, and omelets in the morning ($2-8); salads and sandwiches ($8-11), including a warm chicken panini, at midday. Jazz on the stereo and local art on the walls make it feel cool and arty, and Wi-Fi is free.

CAMPING

The six campgrounds at **Awenda Provincial Park** (Awenda Park Rd., off Concession Rd. 16 E./Lafontaine Rd. E., 888/668-7275, www.ontarioparks.com, mid-May-mid-Oct., reservation fee online $11, by phone $13, tent sites $40, electrical sites $46) are set amid maple and oak forests, so the 333 shaded sites feel comparatively private. All the camping areas have flush toilets and showers, and three have laundry. None of the campgrounds is on the water. The Snake, Wolf, and Deer Campgrounds are closest to the bay, but it's still a long walk. Bring bicycles if you can.

Practicalities

The **Penetanguishene Tourist Information Centre** (2 Main St., 705/549-2232, www.penetanguishene.ca, 9am-6pm daily May-Aug., 10am-6pm daily Sept.-Oct.) is at the town docks. The Midland-Penetanguishene area is about 160 kilometers (100 miles) from Toronto. Highway 93 connects Midland to Penetanguishene, where it becomes Main Street.

★ GEORGIAN BAY ISLANDS NATIONAL PARK

Georgian Bay is dotted with at least 30,000 islands. Some are not much more than a big rock jutting out of the water, while others are substantial enough to house entire communities. A visit to **Georgian Bay Islands National Park** (705/527-7200, www.pc.gc.ca), established in 1929 and encompassing 63 islands across Georgian Bay, is perhaps the easiest way to sample the island experience.

With numerous hiking trails, beaches, and campgrounds as well as a visitors center, Beausoleil Island, the largest of the park's islands, is the most accessible area. Parks Canada runs a seasonal boat service from Honey Harbour to Beausoleil to take day-trippers to the island (in fact, the boat is named

DayTripper). To reach islands other than Beausoleil Island, you need to have your own boat, make arrangements with a local outfitter, or hire a water taxi.

While experienced kayakers and canoeists can explore the park islands on their own, the park service advises extreme caution due to the frequently heavy boat traffic and the many rocks just under the surface that can surprise the unwary. The park has partnered with **White Squall Paddling Centre** (19 James St., Parry Sound, 705/746-4936, www.whitesquall.com) to offer guided kayak trips to some of the park's northern islands.

Honey Harbour is the jumping-off point to visit the park. It's about 168 kilometers (104 miles) northwest of Toronto and 35 kilometers (22 miles) northwest of Midland, the nearest major town. If you don't have a car, you can ride the convenient **Parkbus** (800/928-7101, www.parkbus.ca, adults $57 one-way, $82 round-trip, seniors and students $52 one-way, $74 round-trip, ages 2-12 $29 one-way, $41 round-trip) from Toronto to Honey Harbour on selected summer weekends. The bus departs from several points in Toronto, including 30 Carlton Street (between Yonge St. and Church St., subway: College) and Dufferin Street at Bloor Street West (subway: Dufferin).

Georgian Bay Islands National Park is technically open year-round, but park services, including boat transportation between Honey Harbour and Beausoleil Island, operate only between mid-May and mid-October.

Beausoleil Island

The main destination for visitors exploring Georgian Bay Islands National Park is this 11-square-kilometer (4.2-square-mile) island, 15 minutes by boat from the Parks Canada marina in Honey Harbour. A unique feature of Beausoleil Island is that it encompasses two different natural environments. The northern part of the island is typical of the Canadian Shield, which extends into Northern Ontario, with its rocky shoreline and its windblown juniper and pine forests. On Beausoleil's southern half, you'll see more hardwood trees,

That's a Lot of Islands

Many people outside Ontario know about the Thousand Islands, the chain of islands along the St. Lawrence River in the eastern part of the province. After all, there's even a salad dressing with the Thousand Islands name. Yet the Georgian Bay region has far more than just a thousand isles. Depending on who's counting, Georgian Bay is dotted with at least 30,000 islands. It's one of the world's largest freshwater archipelagoes. Some of these islands are hardly more than specks of bare rock, while others are quite substantial. Manitoulin Island, which measures 2,765 square kilometers (1,067 square miles) on the bay's northern side, is the largest freshwater island in the world.

What created these many different islands? During the ice age, more than 10,000 years ago, glaciers covered what is now Canada. According to one theory, the movement of these glaciers compressed and reshaped the land, fashioning the distinctive landscape of islands and coves that today surrounds Georgian Bay.

UNESCO has recognized the unique geography of the Georgian Bay region and its islands, designating 347,000 hectares (857,455 acres) of the shoreline between the Severn and French Rivers as the **Georgian Bay Biosphere Reserve** (705/774-0978, www.gbbr.ca). One of 15 such reserves in Canada, it's home to more than 100 species of at-risk animals and plants, including the eastern wolf, the lake sturgeon, and the Massasauga rattlesnake. The biosphere's mission is to assist in the conservation of these species and to support education and sustainable development in the region.

The 30,000 Islands are a mix of public and private lands. Some, like the 63 islands of **Georgian Bay Islands National Park** (705/526-9804, www.pc.gc.ca) or **Fathom Five National Marine Park** (519/596-2233, www.pc.gc.ca), are government-protected natural areas. Many others are privately owned, with a cottage or two offering their owners a waterfront getaway. Visitors to this island region can cruise around the bays and harbors, explore the island parks, and even soar above the islands by floatplane. So come back again; to tour even a fraction of these 30,000 islands will take years of exploring.

especially maples, beech, oak, and birch, and land that's grassy or marshy rather than rocky. The best sandy beaches are on the southern end, but you can swim almost anywhere that looks inviting. Bring your own food, water, and anything else you need (hiking shoes, swim suit, towel, and insect repellent). While park rangers are on duty on Beausoleil Island from spring to fall, there are no snack bars or other services.

Beausoleil Island has about a dozen marked hiking trails, including the 6.9-kilometer (4.3-mile) Huron path that runs between the island's north and south and the 2.5-kilometer (1.5-mile) loop around pretty Fairy Lake. Most are for hikers only, but mountain bikes are allowed on two of the routes. For trail details, pick up the free park *Visitor Guide* at any of the park offices or at the Beausoleil welcome center.

Parks Canada runs the **DayTripper** boat (705/526-8907, adults $15.70, seniors $13.45, ages 6-16 $11.70) to transport visitors from Honey Harbour to Beausoleil Island. The *DayTripper* makes the 15-minute trip several times a day in July and August and Friday through Tuesday in the spring and fall. The *DayTripper* rates include park admission. Phone for reservations, which are advised.

Two privately owned water taxis also shuttle visitors from Honey Harbour to the park's islands: **Georgian Bay Water Services** (705/627-3062, www.gbws.ca) and **Honey Harbour Boat Club** (705/756-2411, www.hhbc.ca). If you take a water taxi to Beausoleil, park admission is adults $5.80, seniors $4.90, and ages 6-16 $2.90.

Accommodations and Food

Within the national park, you can camp or stay in one of the camping cabins. Otherwise, you'll need to sleep on the mainland.

CAMPING

Beausoleil Island has nine campgrounds. The largest is **Cedar Spring Campground** (705/526-8907, $25.50, reservation fee $9.80 per campsite), near the boat dock, with 56 tent sites and six family-friendly two-bedroom camping cabins (sleeps up to 5, $160), as well as flush toilets and showers.

In addition to the cabins at Cedar Spring, four lovely secluded **cabins** ($140) overlook the shore at **Christian Beach.** Sleeping two adults, the cabins come with a queen bed, a table and chairs, barbecues, and solar-powered electricity. Park staff transport your gear from the *DayTripper* dock and provide water; the cabins have no plumbing, but there's a composting toilet nearby. Consider bringing or renting a mountain bike, which will give you more flexibility in exploring the island. It's a 1.8-kilometer (1.2-mile) walk from the Cedar Spring boat dock.

If you don't have camping gear or don't want the hassle of transporting it, ask about the park's **equipped camping service** (705/526-8907, reservations required, $55). You get a large prospector tent that staff set up before you arrive, with cots or sleeping pads, along with a dining shelter, a table and chairs, a propane stove, and a water container. Bring sleeping bags or bedding, food, cooking gear, and other personal items.

The island's remaining primitive campgrounds ($15.70) are first-come, first-served with either pit or composting toilets. Campers must bring their own water:

- **Honeymoon Bay** (13 sites), at the island's northernmost end
- **Chimney Bay** (6 sites)
- **The Oaks** (7 sites)
- **Sandpiper** (8 sites)
- **Tonch North** (4 sites)
- **Tonch East** (7 sites)
- **Tonch South** (7 sites)
- **Thumb Point** (8 sites)

OUTSIDE THE PARK

The village of Honey Harbour, where the park boat dock is located, has a handful of seasonal places to stay and eat. Port Severn is a blink-and-you'll-miss-it town off Highway 400's exit 153, just south of the Honey Harbour turnoff, but it has the nicest lodging in the vicinity of the national park. If you want to stay somewhere with more food and entertainment options, sleep in the Midland area and spend the

Christian Beach cabins in the Georgian Bay Islands National Park

day in the national park; it's about an hour's drive.

The closest lodging to the park, **Delawana Inn Resort** (42 Delawana Rd., Honey Harbour, 888/557-0980, www.delawana.ca) has been a summer camp-like property since the 1890s. New owners purchased the resort and resumed limited operations in 2014, while renovations were underway and new programming was in development. Call or check the website for an update.

The **Rawley Resort and Spa** (2900 Kellys Rd., Port Severn, 705/538-2272 or 800/263-7538, www.rawleyresort.com) feels like a waterfront estate, particularly as you sit in the dining room, looking across the manicured lawns to the water. The restaurant is rather formal, serving classic dishes such as veal scaloppini, grilled steak, or roasted Alaskan halibut, with live jazz several nights a week. Accommodations are spread over several buildings and range from upscale guest rooms, to large one- or two-bedroom suites, to two-story loft units overlooking the water. There's an outdoor pool and a small beach.

Information and Services

The administrative office of **Georgian Bay Islands National Park** (705/527-7200, info. gbi@pc.gc.ca, 8am-4pm Mon.-Fri.) is located in Midland. You can phone or email for information year-round. The park service runs a **Welcome Centre** (9:30am-5pm Sun.-Thurs., 9am-7pm Fri., 9am-6pm Sat. July-Aug., 9:30am-5pm Sun.-Tues., 9am-7pm Fri., 9am-6pm Sat. mid-May-June and Sept.-mid-Oct.) on Beausoleil Island, near the Cedar Spring Campground.

At the **Lock 45 Port Severn Welcome Centre** (175 Port Severn Rd. N., Port Severn, 705/538-2586, mid-May-mid-Oct.), off Highway 400's exit 153 between Midland and Honey Harbour, Parks Canada staff provides information about park and area activities. The Welcome Centre is located on the 386-kilometer (240-mile) **Trent-Severn Waterway** that connects Lake Ontario with Georgian Bay; the lock station has a small exhibit area about the waterway and the lock system, and you can watch boats transiting the lock.

PARRY SOUND

Fronting Georgian Bay, Parry Sound is a jumping-off point for exploring the 30,000 Islands region, which dots the waters just offshore. It's a popular destination for kayaking, whether you're just getting started or you're an experienced paddler. For a relatively small community (the year-round population is about 6,000), Parry Sound has a surprisingly robust cultural life, drawing music lovers in particular to the beautifully designed performing arts center.

Parry Sound's most famous native son may be hockey player Bobby Orr, whose legacy lives on in the **Bobby Orr Hall of Fame** (Charles W. Stockey Centre for the Performing Arts, 2 Bay St., 705/746-4466 or 877/746-4466, www. bobbyorrhalloffame.com, 10am-5pm Tues.-Sat., 11am-4pm Sun. July-early Sept., 10am-5pm Wed.-Sat. early Sept.-June; adults $9, seniors and children $6, families $25). The first-floor exhibits document Orr's legendary National Hockey League career, beginning in 1962, when the Boston Bruins recruited him for their junior team at age 14. If you have kids in tow, they'll likely head upstairs to play the hockey skills games.

30,000 Islands Cruises

Off the Parry Sound coast, Georgian Bay is dotted with thousands of islands, and one of the best ways to explore this coastal region is on a cruise. The 550-passenger *Island Queen* (9 Bay St., 705/746-2311 or 800/506-2628, www.islandqueencruise.com), which bills itself as Canada's largest sightseeing boat, runs a three-hour cruise (1pm daily June-mid-Oct., adults $38, ages 6-12 $19) that passes Killbear Provincial Park and circles a number of the islands. In July and August, there's also a two-hour morning cruise (10am daily July-Aug., adults $28, ages 6-12 $14) that sticks closer to shore and the inner islands, where you can catch glimpses of cottages and vacation homes.

After years of service as Niagara Falls' *Maid of the Mist,* the **MV *Chippewa III*** (Spirit of the Sound Schooner Co., Seguin River Parkette, off Bay St., 705/746-6064 or 888/283-5870, www.spiritofthesound.ca, July-Aug.) tours the waters off Parry Sound. They offer a variety of island cruises, including a two-hour afternoon cruise (adults $26, under age 17 $13), a sunset cocktail cruise (adults $30, under age 17 $15), and a dinner cruise (adults $60, under age 15 $4 per year). They also run trips to **Henry's Fish Restaurant** (705/746-9040, mid-May-Sept.) on Frying Pan Island (adults $38, under age 17 $19), combining a cruise with a stop for a fish-and-chips lunch.

★ Flight-Seeing

Touring the 30,000 Islands by boat is a lovely way to spend an afternoon, but seeing the islands by air is an entirely different thrill. Run by husband-and-wife pilots Keith and Nicole Saulnier, **Georgian Bay Airways** (11A Bay St., 705/774-9884 or 800/786-1704, www.georgianbayairways.com, May-Oct.) flies Cessna floatplanes that take off from Parry Sound Harbor and soar over the nearby islands. Seeing the islands from above gives you a much clearer picture of their number and diversity; some are barely more than a boulder in the bay, while others support entire towns. Keith and Nicole know the region well and can tell you all about the islands below.

The basic tour runs 25-35 minutes (adults $103-135), or you can opt for a variety of special flights, from a sunset champagne flight ($310 per couple) to a fish-and-chips meal at **Henry's Fish Restaurant** (705/746-9040, mid-May-Sept.) on Frying Pan Island. They've hosted in-flight marriage proposals, and even a wedding, so if you have something special in mind, let them know.

Canoeing and Kayaking

The Parry Sound area is an excellent starting point for canoe or kayak tours, and one well-established local outfitter has two locations to help you get out on the water. The **White Squall Paddling Centre** (53 Carling Bay Rd., Nobel, 705/342-5324, www.whitesquall.com, 9am-5:30pm Sat.-Thurs., 9am-8pm Fri. Apr.-Aug., 9am-5:30pm daily Sept.-mid-Oct.), on Cole Lake, rents canoes and kayaks, offers lessons that including stand-up paddleboarding, and organizes a variety of day-trips as well as multiday kayak tours. It's located off Highway 559 en route to Killbear Provincial Park.

In downtown Parry Sound, the **White**

The M.V. *Chippewa III* cruises the waters near Parry Sound.

Squall Outdoor Gear Store (19 James St., 705/746-4936, www.whitesquall.com, 9:30am-5:30pm Mon.-Thurs. and Sat., 9:30am-8pm Fri., 11am-4pm Sun. summer) is primarily a gear shop, but you can get information about rentals and trips here, too.

Entertainment and Shopping

The hub of cultural life in Parry Sound—indeed, in this entire region of Ontario—is the **Charles W. Stockey Centre for the Performing Arts** (2 Bay St., 705/746-4466 or 877/746-4466, www.stockeycentre.com). This striking contemporary building, right on the bay and built of local timber and stone, hosts concerts, lectures, and other events year-round. Parry Sound's major cultural event, held at the Stockey Centre, is the annual **Festival of the Sound** (42 James St., 705/746-2410 or 866/364-0061, www.festivalofthesound.ca). Since 1979, this classical-music festival has been drawing Canadian and international musicians and music lovers for three weeks of concerts in July and August.

Accommodations

Parry Sound has several B&Bs and small inns located between downtown and the harbor. The nicest spots to relax at the homey and well-located **40 Bay Street Bed & Breakfast** (40 Bay St., 705/746-9247 or 866/371-2638, www.40baystreet.com, $150-200 d) are the two sunporches overlooking the harbor. The Bay Room, the smallest of the three cozy guest quarters (all with private baths), has expansive harbor views, too. The Retreat Room's special feature is the oversize bath, and the Garden Room lives up to its name with a private deck facing the flower-filled yard. No kids under age 11.

You have plenty of space to unwind at **Victoria Manor Bed & Breakfast** (43 Church St., 705/774-1125, www.victoriamanorbb.ca, $108 d), constructed in 1907, with a traditional parlor, cozy book-lined library, and large screened porch. Upstairs, three comfortable guest rooms have individual touches: the Blue Room has a private deck,

the Red room has an antique washbasin, and the bay-windowed Pink Room features an elaborately quirky lamp. Though the rooms share one large bath, guests sign up for their morning shower time to minimize congestion. The B&B is a short walk from downtown.

Built in 1882 (with a 1950s addition), the rambling 11-room **Bayside Inn** (10 Gibson St., 705/746-7720 or 866/833-8864, www.psbaysideinn.com, $128-143 d) is conveniently located near downtown. The well-turned-out rooms, done in a modern country style, all have air-conditioning, flat-screen TVs, Wi-Fi, and refrigerators. For families, ask for a room with two sleeping areas separated by a divider. Free coffee and tea are available every morning, and guests can have breakfast for a small additional charge (continental $4, full breakfast $8).

Though rustic on the outside, the six units (in three cabins) overlooking the river at the **Log Cabin Inn** (9 Little Beaver Blvd., at Oastler Park Dr., 705/746-7122, www.logcabininn.net, $150 d) are country-contemporary inside, with a king or two queen beds, fireplaces, and modern baths. Rates include continental breakfast, and packages including breakfast and dinner in the upscale restaurant are available. The property is three kilometers (1.9 miles) south of town.

Food

The downtown area, around the intersection of Seguin and James Streets, has several basic places to eat. Along the harbor, Bay Street has a couple of seasonal eateries, open in the summer and fall.

Families and couples, visitors and locals, even the occasional visiting hockey team all turn up at **Wellington's Pub and Grill** (105 James St., 705/746-1333, www.wellingtonspubandgrill.com, $10-25), a friendly pub-restaurant downtown decorated with black-and-white photos from Parry Sound's past. From salads to steaks to succulent schnitzel, the food is straightforward but tasty, and the bar stocks plenty of local brews.

For more gourmet dining, head south of

Two More Georgian Bay Parks

Traveling along Highway 69 north of Parry Sound, you'll find two more provincial parks that are worth a stop for an afternoon, a weekend, or more: Grundy Lake and French River.

GRUNDY LAKE PROVINCIAL PARK

The family-friendly outdoor destination **Grundy Lake Provincial Park** (20400 Hwy. 522, Britt, 705/383-2286, www.ontarioparks.com, mid-May-mid-Oct., $14.50 per vehicle) is filled with lakes, and not just the one that gives the park its name. The forests, wetlands, rocky shores, and sandy beaches feel less wild, at least in the front country, than in the parks fronting Georgian Bay, but Grundy Lake has a gentle beauty and plenty to do.

The park's **Interpretive Centre** at Smokey Point offers summer nature programs, guided hikes, and other activities for kids. You can swim from sandy Main Beach on Grundy Lake and from the seven other **beaches** around the park, and the calm waters make for peaceful canoeing and kayaking. Though the park doesn't rent boats, **Grundy Lake Supply Post** (Hwy. 69 at Hwy. 522, Britt, 705/383-2251, www.grundylakesupplypost.com, 8am-9pm daily July-early Sept., 8am-5pm Mon.-Sat., 9am-5pm Sun. mid-May-June and early Sept.-mid-Oct.) does, and they'll deliver **canoes** ($30-35 per day) and **kayaks** ($30 per day) to the park.

For **hiking**, the park has several moderate trails. The 2.5-kilometer (1.5-mile) Gut Lake Trail follows the rock-lined shore that's part of the Canadian Shield, while the 1.5-kilometer (0.9-mile) Swan Lake Trail wanders through the marshlands around Swan Lake. On the 3.6-kilometer (2.25-mile) Beaver Dams Trail, you'll see the dams that give the path its name; park staff report that hikers have spotted deer, grouse, and even moose on this trail.

Campers can choose from 586 sites across nine **campgrounds** (tent sites $40-44, electrical sites $46-50). Most have sites on or near a lakeshore, with showers, flush toilets, and laundry facilities nearby. Grundy Lake offers Ontario Parks's **Learn to Camp** program on several summer weekends. The park provides tents, air mattresses, a camp stove, cooking equipment, and firewood, and staff teach you the basics for getting started outdoors, from pitching a tent to building a campfire. Grundy also runs two-hour **Learn to Fish** programs, where you learn fundamental fishing skills and then go out to catch your own.

town to the **Log Cabin Inn** (9 Little Beaver Blvd., at Oastler Park Dr., 705/746-7122, www.logcabininn.net, lunch $8-15, dinner $23-40), where you can sample apple-wood-smoked pork chops, pan-seared pickerel, or filet mignon in, yes, a log cabin. Don't expect pioneer hardship, though; the solid log structure with a soaring ceiling overlooks the river, with a fireplace, twinkling candles, and a lengthy wine list setting the mood.

Information and Services

Georgian Bay Country Tourism (70 Church St., 705/746-1287 or 888/229-7257, www.gbcountry.com) can provide information about the Parry Sound region. Parry Sound is 222 kilometers (138 miles) northwest of Toronto along Highway 400/69. It's 163 kilometers (101 miles) south of Sudbury via Highway 69, and 170 kilometers (105 miles) from Killarney.

Getting There and Around

Ontario Northland (800/461-8558, www.ontarionorthland.ca) runs three buses daily in each direction between Toronto and Parry Sound (3.5 hours, adults $53) and between Parry Sound and Sudbury (2-2.5 hours, adults $37). Buses stop at Richard's Coffee (119 Bowes St., 705/746-9611), about 1.8 kilometers (1.1 miles) east of downtown. Two or three times a week, **VIA Rail** (888/842-7245, www.viarail.ca) runs the *Canadian* between Vancouver and Toronto; it stops at Parry Sound Train Station (70 Church St.), about one kilometer (0.6 miles) north of downtown,

Grundy Lake is 85 kilometers (53 miles) north of Parry South and about 20-minutes' drive south of the Highway 637 turnoff for Killarney Provincial Park.

FRENCH RIVER PROVINCIAL PARK

The French River, which runs 110 kilometers (68 miles) from Lake Nipissing to Georgian Bay, was an aboriginal trading route for thousands of years before the first French explorers and missionaries arrived in the early 1600s. The river became an important passage for the fur trade in the 1700s and early 1800s. **French River Provincial Park** (705/857-1630, www.ontarioparks.com) incorporates part of this territory, and it's a good place to take a break along Highway 69. The park **Visitors Centre** (daily July-Aug., Sat.-Sun. late-May-June and Sept.-mid-Oct., $2), in an interesting modern building, has a *Voices of the River* exhibit about the area's history, particularly the mix of First Nations, French, and English cultures.

A short walk from the Visitors Centre, a suspension bridge soars over the French River. It's the **world's largest snowmobile bridge**, measuring 156 meters (512 feet) long, built in 2005 by the French River Snow Voyageurs Snowmobile Club. The bridge has great views up and down the river. The four-kilometer (2.5-mile) **Recollet Falls Trail,** which starts at the Visitors Centre, follows the French River Gorge to the waterfall, a route that First Nations people, fur traders, and other explorers would have traveled centuries ago. If you want to stay a while, the park has 230 backcountry campsites. There's no road access to any of the sites, so you need to backpack or paddle in.

French River Provincial Park is about 15 minutes' drive from Grundy Lake. It's 90 kilometers (56 miles) north of Parry Sound and 65 kilometers (40 miles) south of Sudbury.

NO CAR, NO PROBLEM

If you don't have a car, or if you don't want the hassle of driving, check the schedule for the **Parkbus** (800/928-7101, www.parkbus.ca, adults $60 one-way, $86 round-trip, seniors and students $54 one-way, $77 round-trip, ages 2-12 $30 one-way, $43 round-trip), which can take you from Toronto directly to either of these parks on selected weekends.

but the schedule is much less convenient than the bus. Parry Sound's attractions are clustered along the harbor, a short walk from downtown. For taxi service, try **Parry Sound Taxi** (705/746-1221).

★ KILLBEAR PROVINCIAL PARK

With pink granite cliffs, windblown pines, and several long sandy beaches along Georgian Bay, **Killbear Provincial Park** (35 Killbear Park Rd., Nobel, 705/342-5492, www.ontarioparks.com, $14.50 per vehicle) is a spectacular location for outdoor activities such as hiking, canoeing, and swimming. Lesser known than Ontario's "destination" provincial parks like Algonquin or Killarney, Killbear is less than an hour's drive from Parry Sound, which makes it an easy day trip. If you'd like to stay longer, Killbear's campgrounds are the third largest in the Ontario provincial park system; only Algonquin and The Pinery have more campsites.

The park **Visitors Centre** (705/342-5492, 10am-5pm daily mid-May-mid-Oct.) has exhibits about the geology, natural history, and cultural history of the Killbear area. Particularly popular with the kids (well, with most of them) are the snake exhibits; in summer, naturalists give "snake talks" where you can learn about and touch local reptiles. In July and August, you can join in guided hikes, slide shows, kids' activities, and or other interpretive programs. Be sure to walk around to the back of the Visitors Centre for great views of Georgian Bay.

Killbear is home to the endangered Massasuaga rattlesnake. While it's not likely you'll see one, if you do come upon a rattlesnake near the campgrounds or along the road, notify a park staff member, who will relocate the snake to a less-traveled area. Don't try to pick up or move the snake yourself.

The park is officially open mid-May through mid-October, but in the off-season, you can walk in for winter hiking, cross-country skiing, or snowshoeing.

Sports and Recreation

Several easy hiking trails run through the park, making Killbear pleasant for novice hikers. Heading along the shoreline out to the far end of the park, the **Lighthouse Point Trail** is an easy one-kilometer (0.6-mile) route that passes a 1904 lighthouse. The 3.5-kilometer (2.2-mile) **Lookout Point Trail** goes through the forest to a lookout above Georgian Bay. For the bayside views of the park's pink granite rocks, follow the **Twin Points Trail,** a 1.6-kilometer (1-mile) path loop from the day-use parking area. A six-kilometer (3.7-mile) walking and cycling trail runs from the park entrance past several of the campgrounds to Lighthouse Point.

Killbear's three kilometers (1.9 miles) of sandy beaches include a popular swimming beach at the day-use area. You can swim near most of the campgrounds as well. **Harold Point,** with both a sand beach and rocky cliffs, is a pretty spot to watch the sunset.

Surrounded by water on three sides, Killbear is popular for canoeing and kayaking. The most sheltered waters are near the park's day-use area. Canoe and kayak rentals are not available inside the park, but you can rent boats by the day from nearby outfitters from mid-May to mid-October, including **Killbear Park Mall** (495 Hwy. 559, Nobel, 705/342-5747, www.killbearparkmall.com, canoes $24, single kayaks $29, double kayaks $45, stand-up paddleboards $29) and **The Detour Store** (401 Hwy. 559, Nobel, 705/342-1611, www.thedetourstore.ca, canoes $22-28, single kayaks $25-30,

double kayaks $35-40). **White Squall Paddling Centre** (53 Carling Bay Rd., Nobel, 705/342-5324, www.whitesquall.com), off Highway 559 en route to Killbear, rents a variety of canoes ($42-47 per day), kayaks (single $24-50 per day, double $33-72 per day), and stand-up paddleboards ($24-33 per day), and runs a shuttle service to deliver boats to locations in and around the park.

Camping

Killbear Provincial Park (35 Killbear Park Rd., Nobel, 705/342-5492, www.ontarioparks.com, tent sites $40-44, electrical sites $46-50) has seven different campgrounds, with a total of 880 campsites, most within a five-minute walk of the shore. All the campgrounds, except for the more remote 55-site Granite Saddle area, have restrooms, showers, and laundry facilities. About one-quarter of the sites have electrical hookups. Among the prime sites are the waterfront campsites fronting the beach at **Kilcoursie Bay.** Other campgrounds with waterfront sites include **Beaver Dams, Harold Point,** and **Lighthouse Point.**

Killbear's campgrounds book up early, so make reservations well in advance through **Ontario Parks Reservation Service** (888/668-7275, www.ontarioparks.com, reservation fee online $11, by phone $13). You can make reservations up to five months before your stay.

Information and Services

Contact the **Killbear Provincial Park office** (35 Killbear Park Rd., Nobel, 705/342-5492, www.ontarioparks.com) or check online with **Friends of Killbear** (www.friendsofkillbear.com) for more information. Several small stores along Highway 559 stock food and other provisions. For a better selection, do your shopping in Parry Sound.

Getting There and Around

By road, Killbear Provincial Park is 35

kilometers (22 miles) northwest of Parry Sound, about a 45-minute drive. From Parry Sound, take Highway 69 north to Nobel, where you pick up Highway 559 west to the park. There's no public transportation to or around the park, so you'll need to come by car.

Killarney

Located on Georgian Bay south of Sudbury, Killarney ranks among Ontario's most beautiful natural destinations. This wilderness park juts out into the bay with white dolomite ridges and pink granite cliffs providing a striking backdrop for hiking, canoeing, and kayaking.

★ KILLARNEY PROVINCIAL PARK

One of Ontario's premier outdoor destinations, **Killarney Provincial Park** (Hwy. 637, Killarney, 705/287-2900, www.ontarioparks.com, $14.50 per vehicle) is known for its striking scenery, particularly the white quartzite and pink granite cliffs that dominate the hilly ridges throughout the park. Dense pine forests surround more than 40 crystal blue lakes, and the park is home to approximately 100 bird species. Killarney's rolling hills are what remains of the La Cloche Mountains. Worn down over millions of years, the La Cloche range once had peaks taller than the present-day Rockies. Today, white rocks peek out through the woods near the peaks, and the granite cliffs that surround many of the lakes and the shores of Georgian Bay glow with a pinkish cast, particularly in the early-morning and late-afternoon sun.

At 645 square kilometers (250 square miles), Killarney is tiny compared to mammoth Algonquin Provincial Park. Yet it feels more remote, with secluded wilderness territory just a short hike or paddle away. This wilderness naturally takes some effort to reach. The park is located off Highway 69 between Parry Sound and Sudbury. Within the park, services are limited and camping is the only accommodations option, although lodgings,

restaurants, and services are located nearby in the village of Killarney.

For most Killarney visitors, the first stop is **George Lake** (off Hwy. 637), where the main park office and campground are located. You can swim or canoe here, and it's the starting point for two of the park's hiking trails. At the **Killarney Park Observatory** (George Lake), evening astronomy programs are held regularly in summer. The park hosts other summer events, from nature presentations to concerts, at the George Lake Amphitheatre. Get schedules from the park office or the **Friends of Killarney Park** (www.friendsofkillarneypark.ca).

Killarney Provincial Park is open year-round, but many businesses in the village close from mid-October to May. And at any time of year, be prepared for sudden storms and rapid weather changes. Even if it's sunny when you head out in the morning, a storm can blow in by afternoon.

Beaches

Killarney's most accessible swimming beaches are two sandy stretches along George Lake. The main beach at **George Lake** is in the day-use area; it's a launching point for canoes and kayaks, so just watch for paddling traffic. **Second Beach** is in the George Lake Campground. You can also swim in the park's numerous interior lakes and rivers.

Canoeing and Kayaking

George Lake is the park's most popular spot for short canoe excursions. You can easily paddle for an hour or two, appreciating the striking scenery, with pink granite cliffs surrounding sections of the lake. **Bell Lake,** on the park's east side, is another good canoeing spot. From the Bell Lake Road turnoff from Highway 637—21 kilometers (13 miles) east of George Lake or 38 kilometers (24 miles) west of Highway 69—it's about nine kilometers (5.5 miles) farther to the lake. Other kayaking destinations include **Chikanishing Creek** (Chikanishing Rd., off Hwy. 637) and areas along Georgian Bay.

Killarney Outfitters (1076 Hwy. 637, 705/287-2828 or 888/222-3410, www.killarneyoutfitters.com) and **Killarney Kanoes** (Bell Lake, 705/287-2197 or 888/461-4446, www.killarneykanoes.com) rent canoes and kayaks at both George and Bell Lakes.

With more than 40 lakes throughout the park, Killarney is a launching point for multiday canoe trips. Killarney Outfitters offers a trip-planning service ($95) that includes suggesting a route, arranging for permits, and preparing a detailed trip plan. They provide gear packages ($84-95 pp per day) for multiday canoe or kayak trips, including canoe or kayak rental, camping gear, and cooking equipment. Another service is a shuttle for canoeists whose excursions start at one point and end at another. Killarney Kanoes can also outfit you for a multiday canoe, kayak, or backpacking adventure.

Based in Parry Sound, the **White Squall Paddling Centre** (705/746-4936 or 705/342-5324, www.whitesquall.com) is another outfitter that organizes multiday kayak trips in the Killarney area.

Hiking

Killarney Provincial Park isn't really a beginner's hiking destination, but the park rates several of the trails "moderate," suitable for people who can manage some steep sections and rocky terrain. Hiking times are estimates only; it's a good idea to talk with park staff before you head out.

Across the highway from the George Lake park office, you can pick up the **Granite Ridge Trail,** which winds through the forest and climbs up to two lookout points, one overlooking Georgian Bay and the other onto the rocky cliffs of La Cloche Range. Allow 1

to 1.25 hours for this moderate two-kilometer (one-mile) loop trail. The longer **Cranberry Bog Trail** (four kilometers, 2.5 miles) starts in the George Lake Campground; the trailhead is near site no. 101. As the name suggests, it passes through bogs and marshes, and then goes along A. Y. Jackson Lake, named for one of the Group of Seven artists. Allow about two hours round-trip.

A short hike that gives you beautiful views of Georgian Bay's rocky shores is the **Chikanishing Trail.** Allow 1 to 1.5 hours for this three-kilometer (1.9-mile) loop that involves some scrambles across massive granite boulders (best save this hike for a dry day, as the rocks can be slippery when wet). The trailhead is at the end of Chikanishing Road, off Highway 637 about two kilometers (1.2 miles) west of George Lake.

For great vistas across the La Cloche Mountains, climb up through the boulders of **The Crack,** a challenging but rewarding trail. This six-kilometer (3.7-mile) route has difficult, rocky sections, and the trail is not a loop, so you must return the same way you came in. Pick up the trail off Highway 637, seven kilometers (4.3 miles) east of the George Lake park office. Save this hike for a clear day to appreciate the awesome views. The trail to The Crack is part of the 100-kilometer (62-mile) **La Cloche Silhouette Trail,** a difficult backpacking route that will take many hikers at least seven days.

On the east side of the park, the **Lake of the Woods Trail** is a 3.5-kilometer (2.2-mile) loop around Lake of the Woods; part of the route crosses a beaver dam. The trail starts from Bell Lake Road, which is off Highway 637, about 21 kilometers (13 miles) east of George Lake or 38 kilometers (24 miles) west of Highway 69.

Art Programs

If Killarney's natural setting inspires you to make art, look for details about the **Artist-in-Residence Program.** Created by the Friends of Killarney Park, this summer program brings an established artist to the park to work and offer classes to visitors. Check with the park office or the Friends of Killarney Park website (www.friendsofkillarneypark.ca) for details about these art experiences.

Skiing and Snowshoeing

The park has more than 30 kilometers (19 miles) of trails for cross-country skiing and snowshoeing. The trails all start at the George Lake Park Office, which also offers snowshoe rentals. You can usually expect plenty of snow December through March.

Camping

Killarney's car-camping area is the **George Lake Campground** (July-mid-Oct. $44, mid-Oct.-June $35), which has 128 campsites, with flush toilets, showers (July-mid-Oct.), and laundry facilities, but no electricity. The most secluded spots are near Second Beach, along Blue Heron Circle, although those sites are also the farthest from the showers.

To reserve a campsite, contact **Ontario Parks Reservations** (888/668-7275, www.ontarioparks.com, reservation fee online $11, by phone $13) up to five months in advance; early reservations are recommended, particularly for summer weekends. Campsites can be reserved from May to October; the rest of the year, sites are first-come, first-served.

The George Lake Campground also has six **yurts** (year-round, reservations required, $98). Aluminum-framed yurts sleep up to six, have two bunk beds with a double lower and single upper bunk, a table and chairs, and electric heat. The adjacent deck has a propane-fueled barbecue and a bear-proof box for storing your food. It's a few-minutes' walk from the yurt parking area (spring-fall); each yurt has a cart for hauling your gear. In winter, so you must ski or snowshoe 500 meters (0.3 miles) from the front gate. Toilets and water taps are located near the parking area.

For a true wilderness experience, head for one of Killarney's year-round **backcountry campsites** (705/287-2900, www.ontarioparks.com, adults $12, ages 6-17 $5.10). You can hike in to 33 of these sites; another 140 backcountry campsites are accessible only by canoe.

Killarney Kanoes (Bell Lake, 705/287-2197 or 888/461-4446, www.killarneykanoes.com) rents tents, sleeping bags, and other camping gear.

The Village of Killarney

About 500 people live in the village of

view from the top of The Crack trail at Killarney Provincial Park

Killarney, which is on the harbor 10 kilometers (six miles) west of the provincial park. Until 1962, when Highway 637 was built between Killarney and Highway 69, the only way to get to the village was by water (or in winter, across the ice to Manitoulin Island). Killarney was originally known by its Ojibwa name, Shebahonaning, and many present-day residents have aboriginal roots.

Most of the town's lodgings and services are located on or near Channel Street, named for the Killarney Channel, which the street follows. The nicest time to stroll along the waterfront is in the early evening, as the sun begins to set. The land you see directly across the channel is George Island. Formerly a logging area, the island is now primarily wilderness. You can hike around the island on the 7.5-kilometer (4.7-mile) **George Island Trail,** which is rated moderate to difficult; make sure you have sturdy hiking boots and enough food and water for the day. Both the **Killarney Mountain Lodge** (705/287-2242, www.killarney.com) and the Sportsman's Inn (705/287-9990, www.sportsmansinn.ca) arrange boat transportation to and from George Island.

Originally built in 1868 and rebuilt in 1909, the **Killarney East Lighthouse** (Ontario St.) is at the mouth of the channel on the east side of the village. You can hike or swim nearby, and it's especially pretty just before sunset.

ACCOMMODATIONS AND FOOD

None of the places to stay in the village of Killarney are particularly upscale, but most are comfortable enough and have restaurants or pubs. Many accommodations and other services close between mid-October and early May.

Opposite the harbor, **The Pines Inn** (36 Channel St., 705/287-1068, www.bbcanada.com, year-round, $90-95 s or d) is a comfortable, old-time lodge with a busy pub and restaurant. Upstairs, the six simple guest rooms with quilt-covered beds share two baths; washbasins in the rooms help minimize the wait. Owners Paul and Adele Malcew offer a

warm welcome, with Paul serving cold beer behind the bar and Adele cooking bacon-and-eggs breakfasts, burgers, grilled fish, and other home-style fare. Even if you're not staying here, stop in for a drink and a chat; the pub is a local hangout.

At the **Sportsman's Inn** (37 Channel St., 705/287-9990 or 877/333-7510, www.sportsmansinn.ca, mid-May-mid-Oct.) on the harbor, there are several different room types, from plain rooms in a separate motel building ($109 d) to more upscale units overlooking the waterfront ($159 d) to large two-bedroom suites ($320 d). The main dining room serves straightforward traditional fare, from grilled chicken to whitefish to steak ($20-29), while the pub sticks with nachos, burgers, and other basics.

A holiday at the waterfront ★ **Killarney Mountain Lodge** (3 Commissioner St., 705/287-2242 or 800/461-1117, www.killarney.com, mid-May-mid-Oct., $75 s, $150 d with breakfast, $120-195 pp with breakfast and dinner, $135-195 pp with 3 meals), with rustic pine-paneled rooms and cabins, a pool, games, and canoes, feels summer camp. The dining room serves three basic meals daily, and there's live music (from 9pm Tues.-Sun.) in the window-lined **Carousel Bar.** TV and Wi-Fi are in the main lodge, but rooms have no phones, TVs, or Internet access. The owners also operate Killarney Outfitters store and guide service; ask about packages including activities.

Lines are legendary at **Herbert Fisheries** (21 Channel St., 705/287-2214, lunch and dinner daily June-Aug., Fri.-Sun. May and Sept.-early Oct.), which serves first-rate fish-and-chips (from $16) on the waterfront.

Information and Services

When you arrive in the Killarney area, stop at the **Killarney Provincial Park** main office (Hwy. 637, 705/287-2900) at George Lake to pick up the free park information guide and ask questions of the park staff. The **Friends of Killarney Park Store** (George Lake Campground, 705/287-2800, www.

friendsofkillarneypark.ca, year-round) sells park guides, maps, books, and other souvenirs; they have a second location at Bell Lake. You can also order canoeing and hiking guides online—a boon for trip planning.

The useful website of **Friends of Killarney Park** (www.friendsofkillarneypark.ca) has information about park events, hiking trails, and other activities. The Friends also run an online forum, where you can post questions about hiking and canoe trips and read trip reports from others who have explored the park.

The **Killarney Outfitters Store** (1076 Hwy. 637, 705/287-2828 or 888/222-3410, www.killarneyoutfitters.com, 8am-8pm daily July-Aug., 8am-5pm daily spring and fall) is located between the village and the main park entrance at George Lake. They sell outdoor clothing and camping supplies; rent canoes and kayaks ($37-59) as well as other gear; and can arrange a variety of outdoor excursions. **Pitfield's General Store** (7 Channel St., 705/287-2872) sells basic groceries and snacks year-round. They also have a coin laundry.

Getting There and Around
CAR
Killarney is 425 kilometers (265 miles) northwest of Toronto, about a 5-6-hour

drive. Sudbury is the closest city, about a 90-minute drive to the north; Parry Sound is two hours' drive to the south. The only road into Killarney is Highway 637, which is off Highway 69 between Parry Sound and Sudbury. From the Highway 69/637 interchange, it's 67 kilometers (42 miles) to the village of Killarney, about an hour by car.

While the village of Killarney is only about 20 nautical miles from the eastern tip of Manitoulin Island, there's no public boat service between the two. By car, it's a three-hour drive from Killarney to Little Current (220 kilometers, 137 miles). From Killarney, return to Highway 69 and travel north toward Sudbury; then take Highway 17 west to Espanola, where you pick up Highway 6 south, which crosses the bridge to Manitoulin.

BUS
Without a car, the simplest way to travel from Toronto to Killarney is on the **Parkbus** (800/928-7101, www.parkbus.ca, one-way adults $64, seniors and students $58, ages 2-12 $32, round-trip adults $92, seniors and students $83, ages 2-12 $46), which operates on selected weekends in summer and fall. The bus departs from several points in Toronto, including 30 Carlton Street (between Yonge

Killarney Mountain Lodge has plenty of spots to relax.

St. and Church St., subway: College) and Dufferin Street at Bloor Street West (subway: Dufferin). The Parkbus picks up and drops off at three points in the Killarney area: Bell Lake, George Lake (at the park headquarters and main campground), and in the village of Killarney. The Parkbus also works with local outfitters to offer all-inclusive packages, including transportation and lodging; get details on the website.

Otherwise, it's not easy to get to Killarney without a car. **Ontario Northland** (www. ontarionorthland.ca) buses between Parry Sound and Sudbury will stop at Highway 637, but you're still an hour's drive from town or the park. **Killarney Outfitters** (705/287-2828 or 888/222-3410, www.killarneyoutfitters.com) can provide a shuttle ($130 one-way) from the bus stop into town, which is pricey unless you can split the cost among travelers.

Manitoulin Island

Bordered by Lake Huron to the west and Georgian Bay to the east, Manitoulin isn't Canada's largest island (that distinction belongs to Baffin Island). Yet Manitoulin is still tops for its size: It's the largest freshwater island in the world.

Don't expect to make a quick loop around Manitoulin in a couple of hours. Measuring 2,765 square kilometers (1,067 square miles), with good but meandering roads, Manitoulin is a place for leisurely exploration. One of the most significant things to explore is the island's aboriginal culture. Manitoulin and the surrounding mainland region are home to eight First Nations, collectively known as the Anishinaabe people. An innovative aboriginal tourism association, the **Great Spirit Circle Trail,** offers a variety of cultural programs to introduce visitors to local First Nations traditions. The First Nations communities hold traditional **powwows** that welcome visitors, too.

Because the island is so large, consider your interests in deciding where to stay. If you're interested in aboriginal culture, base yourself on the island's eastern half, where you'll be close to more First Nations attractions. For the best beaches, head south; the nicest sandy spot is Providence Bay on the south shore. And if you're looking for a remote getaway, go west, where villages like Gore Bay and Meldrum Bay have comfortable inns.

Scientists believe that millions of years ago, Manitoulin was connected by land to the Bruce Peninsula. Today, the only land access is from the north, via Highway 6, where a "**swing bridge**"—similar to a drawbridge, except that it swings sideways instead of lifting—links the island to the mainland.

If you're coming from Toronto and Southern Ontario, the most direct route to Manitoulin is by boat. From mid-May to mid-October, a ferry runs between Tobermory, on the Bruce Peninsula, and South Baymouth, on the southeast corner of Manitoulin Island. The island's high season mirrors the ferry schedule, so when the ferry docks for the winter, many Manitoulin lodgings close and restaurants shut down or reduce their hours.

SIGHTS

Just across the swing bridge onto the island is the town of **Little Current.** The small downtown runs along Water Street, with a handful of shops for browsing. You can also stroll along the harbor, which fronts Lake Huron's North Channel, watching the sailboats and the occasional cruise ship.

★ Great Spirit Circle Trail

Based in M'Chigeeng, the **Great Spirit Circle Trail** (5905 Hwy. 540, 705/377-4404 or 877/710-3211, www.circletrail.com), an aboriginal tourism association, offers a

Manitoulin Island

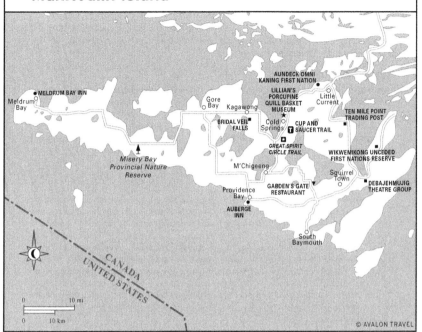

© AVALON TRAVEL

number of activities to introduce visitors to First Nations traditions, and several nearby attractions focus on aboriginal culture. The M'Chigeeng First Nation (the *m* is silent) is 34 kilometers (21 miles) southwest of Little Current and 78 kilometers (48 miles) northwest of South Baymouth.

The Great Spirit Circle Trail offers programs that include one- to two-hour introductions to indigenous herbal medicines, First Nations crafts, storytelling, traditional drumming, longer guided hiking, horseback riding, or canoe experiences. Programs are typically available between late May and early October; call or check the website for details and to make arrangements.

At the **Ojibwe Cultural Foundation and Museum** (15 Hwy. 551, 705/377-4902, www.ojibweculture.ca, 9am-6pm Mon.-Fri., 10am-4pm Sat., noon-4pm Sun. mid-June-Sept., 9am-4:30pm Mon.-Fri. Oct.-mid-June, adults $7.50, seniors and students $5), exhibits

focus on First Nations history and contemporary aboriginal arts.

Opposite the Ojibwe Cultural Foundation, the **Immaculate Conception Church** (Hwy. 551, 705/377-4985, donation) mixes First Nations and Roman Catholic religious traditions. The round structure with a conical roof recalls a traditional tepee; on the bright blue front door, a yellow sun with four rays in the shape of a cross is an indigenous people's religious symbol. Inside, look for other aboriginal paintings and carvings.

Part shop and part gallery, **Lillian's Porcupine Quill Basket Museum** (5950 Hwy. 540, 705/377-4987, www.lillianscrafts. ca, 10am-6pm Mon.-Fri., 10am-5pm Sat.-Sun., free) displays a local First Nations craft: baskets and boxes intricately woven from colorful porcupine quills. Make sure you see the exhibits done by master craftspeople in the back room. The front room sells more typical aboriginal souvenirs.

Planning to Powwow

One of the most interesting ways to experience aboriginal culture is to attend a traditional pow-wow, a festival that encompasses dance, music, and food. And one of Ontario's best places to find powwows is on Manitoulin Island.

WHERE TO POWWOW

Manitoulin's largest and longest-running powwow is the **Wikwemikong Cultural Festival and Powwow** (www.wikwemikongheritage.org), held annually in early August on the Wikwemikong Reserve on the island's east side. Most of Manitoulin's other First Nations communities hold annual traditional powwows, as well, including the **Aundeck Omni Kaning** (June), **Sheguiandah** (July), and **M'Chigeeng** (late Aug. or early Sept.). Get a powwow schedule and details about any of these events from the **Great Spirit Circle Trail office** (705/377-4404 or 877/710-3211, www.circletrail.com).

POWWOW ETIQUETTE

Traditional powwows are generally open to the public, and most are free, although donations are accepted. Competition powwows often charge admission of $10-15. A master of ceremonies leads the powwow and explains the various dances and ceremonies. You can purchase food and traditional crafts on-site.

During certain ceremonial songs or dances, photography and video recording are prohibited; the master of ceremonies will usually explain when these ceremonies are taking place. At other times, you may take photos or videos, but it's polite to ask for permission first, particularly when you're photographing a dancer in traditional regalia. Because many believe that the regalia (which should never be called "costumes") have their own spirit, and frequently are handmade or passed down from an ancestor, you should never touch the regalia, either. Powwows are alcohol-free events.

To learn more about powwow customs and etiquette, request a copy of the Great Spirit Circle Trail's *Powwow Guide* (705/377-4404 or 877/710-3211, www.circletrail.com).

Miigwetch (Thank you)!

Kagawong

Heading west from M'Chigeeng on Highway 540, you reach Kagawong, a cute village whose Ojibwa name means "where mists rise from the falling waters." It's a fitting moniker, since the town's main attraction is **Bridal Veil Falls,** where you can splash under the waterfall. Stairs lead from a parking area down to the falls, and a walking path follows the riverbank from the falls into the village.

If you need a break after playing in the falls, don't worry—there's chocolate. **Manitoulin Chocolate Works** (160 Main St., 705/282-0961, www.manitoulinchocolate.ca, 9am-6pm Mon.-Sat., 11am-5pm Sun. July-Aug., 10am-5pm Tues.-Sat., 11am-4pm Sun. May-June and Sept.-Dec.) crafts chocolates and other confections in a former village blacksmith shop. They sell coffee, tea, and hot chocolate, too.

Sheguiandah and Wikwemikong

South of Little Current along Highway 6, stop at the **Viewpoint at Ten Mile Point,** where vistas stretch east across Sheguiandah Bay. Adjacent to the viewpoint, the **Ten Mile Point Trading Post and Gallery** (12164 Hwy. 6, Sheguiandah, 705/368-2377) looks like a standard souvenir shop, but amid the T-shirts and trinkets are high-quality works, from jewelry to leather to prints, by First Nations artists. They also carry a large selection of books about Manitoulin and First Nations culture, including books for kids.

overlooking the cliffs from the Cup and Saucer Trail

Hiking

One of Manitoulin's most popular hikes is the **Cup and Saucer Trail** (Hwy. 540 at Bidwell Rd., dawn-dusk daily mid-May-mid-Oct.), which climbs the Niagara Escarpment to spectacular lookouts from the 70-meter (230-foot) cliffs. This 12-kilometer (7.5-mile) route is divided into several shorter trails, including the optional two-kilometer (1.2-mile) adventure trail, which takes hikers up and down ladders and along narrow ledges to a viewpoint overlooking the North Channel. The trailhead is 18 kilometers (11 miles) west of Little Current, just north of M'Chigeeng.

A fascinating way to explore the Cup and Saucer Trail is on a **Mother Earth Nature Hike,** (2.5-3 hours, $40 pp) led by an aboriginal guide, who will help you identify local plants and understand how they're used in aboriginal medicine and cooking. Contact the **Great Spirit Circle Trail** (705/377-4404 or 877/710-3211, www.circletrail.com) to book.

Legend has it that, back in the 1880s, a farmer was cutting down grass in southwest Manitoulin when two men approached and asked the place's name. "Misery," the hot, tired farmer called it, and the name stuck. Today, it's the antithesis of misery for hikers who stroll the 15 kilometers (nine miles) of trails in the **Misery Bay Provincial Nature Reserve** (400 Misery Bay Park Rd., 705/966-2315, www.ontarioparks.com and www.miserybay.org, 10am-5pm daily July-Aug., 10am-5pm Sat.-Sun. mid-May-June and Sept.-mid-Oct., adults $2, ages 6-17 $1). The park visitors center has exhibits about the area's geological and natural features, which include its wetlands and its alvar ecosystem, a rare type of flat rock landscape found primarily in the Great Lakes region. You can follow a 1.3-kilometer (0.8-mile) trail to a **swimming beach.** The Misery Bay turnoff is 35 kilometers (22 miles) west of Gore Bay along Highway 540.

On the peninsula jutting out from Manitoulin's eastern shore is the **Wikwemikong Unceded First Nations Reserve**—"unceded" because the group never agreed to any treaty that would give title of its land to the government. It's Canada's only officially recognized unceded aboriginal reserve. The Wikwemikong offer a variety of tours and cultural experiences, including walking tours and canoe excursions. Contact the **Wikwemikong Tourism Information Center** (888/801-9422, www.wikwemikong.ca) for details.

If you visit during July or August, don't miss a production by the **Debajehmujig Theatre Group** (office: 8 Debajehmujig Lane, 705/859-2317, www.debaj.ca). They perform works with aboriginal themes in the ruins of Wikwemikong's Holy Cross Mission and host other theater, music, and art events at their **Debajehmujig Creation Centre** (43 Queen St., Manitowaning, 705/859-1820).

Beaches

Although Manitoulin is ringed with beaches, the best sandy spots are on the south shore, west of South Baymouth. And the best of the best? **Providence Bay Beach,** a long strip of soft sand along Lake Huron, backed by swaying grasses and a boardwalk trail. The beach's Harbour Centre building (spring-fall) has restrooms, a small exhibit area about the local history and environment, and, wonder of wonders, an espresso bar, **Huron Island Time,** run by the owners of the nearby Auberge Inn. It serves coffee, pastries, locally made hot dogs, and ice cream; you can rent kayaks, canoes, bicycles, and beach chairs here as well.

In eastern Manitoulin, off Highway 6 between Sheguiandah and Manitowaning, is the largest of the island's 108 freshwater lakes, Lake Manitou.

ACCOMMODATIONS AND FOOD

Manitoulin lodgings include cottages, B&Bs, small inns, and summer camp-style resorts. No chains or megaresorts have set up shop yet. It's a good idea to book ahead, especially in July and August. Manitoulin isn't a fine-dining destination—it's much easier to find burgers and fish-and-chips than a gourmet meal—but most towns have someplace to get a bite.

Little Current

The Great Spirit Circle Trail runs the 57-room **Manitoulin Hotel and Conference Centre** (66 Meredith St. E., 705/368-9966 or 855/368-9966, www.manitoulinhotel.com or www.circletrail.com, $139-229 d), near the swing bridge. The expansive lobby overlooking the channel is modeled after a First Nations gathering place, and the guest rooms are decorated with light wood furnishings and First Nations' motifs. Amenities include Keurig coffeemakers, flat-screen TVs, and free Wi-Fi.

Both sailors and landlubbers wash into the **Anchor Inn** (1 Water St., 705/368-2023, www.anchorgrill.com, 7am-11pm daily July-Aug., call for off-season hours, lunch $5-15, dinner $8-25) for a beer or for chow that ranges from burgers and sandwiches to steaks and fish plates. Upstairs, the inn has several simple rooms ($50-70 d) and apartments ($80-90 d), although light sleepers should note that rooms over the bar can be noisy, particularly on weekends when bands are playing.

The take-out counter at **Island Jar** (15 Water St., 705/368-1881, 9am-5:30pm

summer fun on Providence Bay Beach

Stay in a teepee on Manitoulin Island.

to the public. For reservations, contact "Our Place" directly, or book through the **Great Spirit Circle Trail** (705/377-4404 or 877/710-3211, www.circletrail.com).

M'Chigeeng

The **Great Spirit Circle Trail** (705/377-4404 or 877/710-3211, www.circletrail.com) has several **tepees** (June-Sept., $40) on their M'Chigeeng property where visitors can stay. Washrooms are a short walk away, and you can rent cots or sleeping bags.

A convenient place to eat before or after you visit the Circle Trail or the Ojibwe Cultural Foundation, **Season's Family Restaurant** (Hwy. 551, 705/377-4344, 7am-7:30pm Mon.-Sat., $5-15) serves bacon and eggs, sandwiches, and other family-style dishes.

South Baymouth and Tehkummah

The closest accommodations to the ferry terminal, the **Southbay Gallery and Guesthouse Manitoulin** (14-15 Given Rd., South Baymouth, 705/859-2363, www.southbayguesthouse.com, May-Sept., $110-169 d) has several guest rooms (two with private baths), with stocky wooden furniture, in two different buildings. The property also includes a self-contained guest cottage, a hot tub, and an art gallery-shop. The same family runs the Southbay Guesthouse in Sudbury.

One of the island's best restaurants is in the countryside 26 kilometers (16 miles) north of South Baymouth. In a house at the end of a garden path, ★ **Garden's Gate Restaurant** (312 Hwy. 542, Tehkummah, 705/859-2088 or 888/959-2088, www.gardensgate.ca, lunch and dinner Tues.-Sun. June, lunch Tues.-Sun. and dinner daily July-Aug., dinner Tues.-Sun. May and Sept.-Oct., lunch $13-15, dinner $16-23), with its floral tablecloths and cozy screened porch, looks grandmotherly, but the food—updated country fare made with fresh local ingredients—is first-rate. Fish is a specialty, and the menu always includes vegetarian options. Save room for the homemade pie.

Mon.-Fri., 9am-5pm Sat.), a small organic grocery, whips up freshly made smoothies, sushi, salads, and sandwiches from pulled pork to hummus. Have coffee and check your email at **Loco Beanz** (7 Water St., 705/368-2261, 7am-5pm Mon.-Sat., 8am-3pm Sun. summer), a cheery café with free Wi-Fi.

Aundeck Omni Kaning

On this First Nations reserve off Highway 540, five kilometers (three miles) west of Little Current, **Endaa-aang "Our Place"** (705/368-0548, www.aokfn.com) rents four well-kept cabins in parklike grounds near the North Channel waterfront. The wood-paneled cabins sleep six, with a double bedroom, a twin-bed room, and a living room with a sofa bed; they have full kitchens as well as decks with barbecues. Also on the property are **tepee rentals.** The tepees sleep eight but are unfurnished. Bring sleeping bags and other camping gear; restrooms are nearby.

Guests can use the reserve's beach along the North Channel, but it's otherwise not open

Providence Bay

A five-minute walk from Providence Bay Beach, the ★ **Auberge Inn** (71 McNevin St., 705/377-4392 or 877/977-4392, www.aubergeinn.ca, year-round, $40 dorm, $95 d), the island's only hostel, is a friendly place with three bunk beds in a dorm and two private rooms, one with a double bed and one with a queen bed and two bunks. Guests share a large bath upstairs. Convivial owners Alain Harvey and Nathalie Gara-Boivin offer great tips and rent bicycles, kayaks, or canoes. Rates include self-serve continental breakfast and Wi-Fi. Nathalie is also a certified yoga teacher, who offers occasional weekend yoga retreats.

What's a day at the beach without fish-and-chips? **Lake Huron Fish and Chips** (20 McNevin St., 705/377-4500, late May-Sept.) is just inland from Providence Bay. Take a peek into their tiny **West Backline Gallery** next door to see what's on view.

Gore Bay

One of Manitoulin's most elegant accommodations is **The Queen's Inn Bed-and-Breakfast** (19 Water St., 705/282-0665, www.thequeensinn.ca, May-Dec., $110-130 s, $135-160 d), overlooking the harbor in Gore Bay. Built in the late 1800s, this Victorian manor has a formal antiques-filled parlor and a saloon-turned-breakfast-room where a hot morning meal is served. On the second and third floors are eight Victorian-style guest rooms, five with private baths. Sit on either of the two verandas to enjoy the harbor views.

Buoys Eatery (1 Purvis Dr., off Water St., 705/282-2869, www.buoyseatery.com, lunch and dinner daily June-Sept., Wed.-Sun. Oct.-May, $9-18) looks like an ordinary fish shack (albeit with a lovely deck), but the two specialties make it worth the stop: fish and wedges (broiled or fried local whitefish paired with thick slices of roasted potato) and pizzas with either traditional or out-of-the-ordinary toppings; the Greek Obsession sports *tzatziki* sauce, gyro meat, feta cheese, and olives.

Meldrum Bay

To get way, way away from it all, book a stay at the family-run **Meldrum Bay Inn** (25959 Hwy. 540, 705/283-3190 or 877/577-1645, www.meldrumbayinn.com, year-round, $140-170 d), in an 1878 wood-frame building with a wide front porch, overlooking the water on Manitoulin's far west end. Seven simple rooms share two baths; rates include continental breakfast. The home-style dining room (late May-mid-Sept., entrées $18-27) specializes in local whitefish and barbecue ribs. Meldrum Bay is 167 circuitous kilometers (104 miles) from South Baymouth and 134 kilometers (83 miles) from Little Current; allow at least two hours from the island's east side.

INFORMATION AND SERVICES

Just over the swing bridge, stop into the **Manitoulin Tourism Association Welcome Centre** (70 Meredith St. E./Hwy. 6, Little Current, 705/368-3021, www.manitoulintourism.com), where obliging staff provide maps and brochures, book ferry reservations, and offer advice about things to do and places to stay. Their website is an excellent resource for planning your island visit; it has a good map with descriptions of Manitoulin's various communities. If you arrive on the ferry, pick up maps and brochures at the **ferry terminal information center** (41 Water St., South Baymouth, 705/859-3161).

For information about aboriginal tourism on Manitoulin, contact the **Great Spirit Circle Trail** (5905 Hwy. 540, M'Chigeeng, 705/377-4404 or 877/710-3211, www.circletrail.com). The **Wikwemikong Tourism Information Center** (888/801-9422, www.wikwemikong.ca) can tell you about activities on the Wikwemikong Reserve.

GETTING THERE
Ferry

From Toronto or other Southern Ontario destinations, the quickest way to Manitoulin is by ferry from the Bruce Peninsula. The **MS *Chi-Cheemaun* Ferry** (800/265-3163, www.ontarioferries.com, mid-May-mid-Oct., one-way adults $16.50, seniors $14.25, ages 5-11 $8.25, cars $27.75-45)—its Ojibwa name means "The Big Canoe"—makes the two-hour run between Tobermory and South Baymouth several times daily. Discounts are available for families and for same-day returns. Make a reservation if you're taking a car; a $15 reservation fee applies to many sailings.

Car

By road, it's a long slog—about 510 kilometers (320 miles) from Toronto to Manitoulin. After taking Highway 400/69 north toward Sudbury, it's still 90 minutes farther on Highway 17 west and Highway 6 south to Manitoulin's **swing bridge.** In summer, every hour on the hour (dawn-dusk), the bridge swings sideways to allow boats to pass underneath, halting road traffic for 15 minutes. The bridge is only one lane, so even when it's open, traffic alternates in each direction. Don't be in a rush to make the crossing.

GETTING AROUND

Highway 6 runs along the island's east side between Little Current and South Baymouth, passing Sheguiandah and Wikwemikong en route. From Little Current, Highway 540 goes west to M'Chigeeng, Kagawong, Gore Bay, and Meldrum Bay. From South Baymouth to M'Chigeeng, take Highway 6 north to Highway 542 west, then, at Mindemoya, pick up Highway 551 north to M'Chigeeng. To Providence Bay, turn south onto Highway 551. For Gore Bay, continue west on Highway 542.

Manitoulin has no public transportation. If you're an avid cyclist able to ride fairly long distances, **bicycling** is a reasonable way to tour the island. From South Baymouth, it's 30 kilometers (19 miles) to Providence Bay and 62 kilometers (39 miles) to Little Current. For cycling tips, check with the **Manitoulin Tourism Association** (705/368-3021, www.manitoulintourism.com) or with the owners of the **Auberge Inn** (71 McNevin, Providence Bay, 705/377-4392 or 877/977-4392, www.aubergeinn.ca).

MAP SYMBOLS

▦	Expressway	★	Highlight	✗	Airfield	⚓	Golf Course
	Primary Road	○	City/Town	✈	Airport	🅿	Parking Area
	Secondary Road	◉	State Capital	▲	Mountain	⬟	Archaeological Site
	Unpaved Road	⊛	National Capital	✛	Unique Natural Feature	♦	Church
	Trail	★	Point of Interest			♨	Gas Station
	Ferry	•	Accommodation	⚲	Waterfall	🗺	Glacier
	Railroad	▼	Restaurant/Bar	▲	Park	🗺	Mangrove
	Pedestrian Walkway	■	Other Location	🚩	Trailhead	🗺	Reef
▥	Stairs	Λ	Campground	🎿	Skiing Area	🗺	Swamp

CONVERSION TABLES

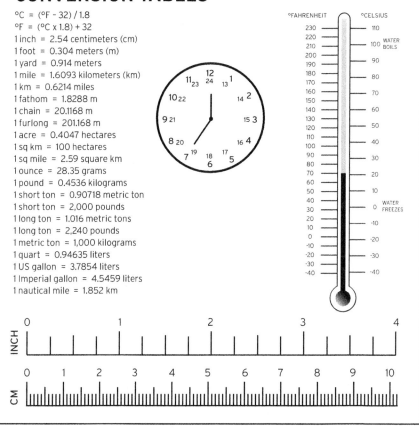

°C = (°F – 32) / 1.8
°F = (°C x 1.8) + 32
1 inch = 2.54 centimeters (cm)
1 foot = 0.304 meters (m)
1 yard = 0.914 meters
1 mile = 1.6093 kilometers (km)
1 km = 0.6214 miles
1 fathom = 1.8288 m
1 chain = 20.1168 m
1 furlong = 201.168 m
1 acre = 0.4047 hectares
1 sq km = 100 hectares
1 sq mile = 2.59 square km
1 ounce = 28.35 grams
1 pound = 0.4536 kilograms
1 short ton = 0.90718 metric ton
1 short ton = 2,000 pounds
1 long ton = 1.016 metric tons
1 long ton = 2,240 pounds
1 metric ton = 1,000 kilograms
1 quart = 0.94635 liters
1 US gallon = 3.7854 liters
1 Imperial gallon = 4.5459 liters
1 nautical mile = 1.852 km

MOON SPOTLIGHT GEORGIAN BAY & COTTAGE COUNTRY

Avalon Travel
a member of the Perseus Books Group
1700 Fourth Street
Berkeley, CA 94710, USA
www.moon.com

Editor: Erin Raber
Copy Editor: Christopher Church
Graphics and Production Coordinator: Darren Alessi
Cover Design: FaceOut Studios, Charles Brock
Moon Logo: Tim McGrath
Map Editor: Kat Bennett
Cartographers: Chris Henrick, Andrea Butkovic, Stephanie Poulain, Brian Shotwell

ISBN: 978-1-63121-095-2

Printed in the United States

ABOUT THE AUTHOR

Carolyn B. Heller

Carolyn B. Heller first visited Ontario as a child. She recalls spending family holidays exploring the Thousand Islands, touring Canada's tomato capital, and cruising under the spray at Niagara Falls. Later, she took her own children to Niagara. After moving to Canada in 2003, Carolyn began scouting out Toronto's neighborhoods, taking in theater festivals at Stratford and Niagara-on-the-Lake, and discovering Ontario's outdoors—from the rocky shores of Bruce Peninsula to the pink cliffs of Killarney and the lakes and trails in Algonquin Provincial Park.

A full-time writer, Carolyn has contributed to more than 50 travel and restaurant guides to destinations ranging from Canada and New England to China. She's the author of *Moon Living Abroad in Canada* and its companion website, www.livingabroadincanada. com. Her articles have appeared in *Forbes* Travel, Viator Travel, the *Los Angeles Times*, *Boston Globe*, *FamilyFun*, *Real Weddings*, and *Perceptive Travel*, as well as the book *Travelers' Tales Paris*.

Carolyn is an avid traveler and passionate food lover who has dined in more than 40 countries. A graduate of Brown University, she lives in Vancouver with her husband and twin daughters. Follow Carolyn's adventures at www.cbheller.com and on Twitter @CarolynBHeller.

CPSIA information can be obtained at www.ICGtesting.com
Printed in the USA
LVOW04s0053300415

436559LV00005B/13/P